SO-DFV-444

RENEWALS 458-4574
DATE DUE

What Does the World
Want from America?

WITHDRAWN
UTSA LIBRARIES

A *WASHINGTON QUARTERLY READER*

What Does the World Want from America?

INTERNATIONAL PERSPECTIVES ON U.S. FOREIGN POLICY

EDITED BY
ALEXANDER T. J. LENNON

THE MIT PRESS
Cambridge, Massachusetts
London, England

The contents of this book were first published in *The Washington Quarterly* (ISSN 0163-660X), a publication of The MIT Press under the sponsorship of The Center for Strategic and International Studies (CSIS). Except as otherwise noted, copyright in each article is owned jointly by the Massachusetts Institute of Technology and CSIS. No article may be reproduced in whole or in part except with the express written permission of The MIT Press.

Wu Xinbo, "To Be an Enlightened Superpower," *TWQ* 24, No. 3 (Summer 2001); Akio Watanabe, "First among Equals," *TWQ* 24, No. 3 (Summer 2001); Kanti Bajpai, "Add Five 'E's to Make a Partnership," *TWQ* 24, No. 3 (Summer 2001); Chong Guan Kwa and See Seng Tan, "The Keystone of World Order," *TWQ* 24, No. 3 (Summer 2001); Francis Kornegay, Chris Landsberg, and Steve McDonald, "Participate in the African Renaissance," *TWQ* 24, No. 3 (Summer 2001); Mahmood Sariolghalam, "Justice for All," *TWQ* 24, No. 3 (Summer 2001); Barry Rubin, "What Is Right Is in U.S. Interests," *TWQ* 24, No. 3 (Summer 2001); Dmitri Trenin, "Less Is More," *TWQ* 24, No. 3 (Summer 2001); Michael Stürmer, "Balance from beyond the Sea," *TWQ* 24, No. 3 (Summer 2001); Pascal Boniface, "The Specter of Unilateralism," *TWQ* 24, No. 3 (Summer 2001); Peter Ludlow, "Wanted: A Global Partner," *TWQ* 24, No. 3 (Summer 2001); Maria Claudia Drummond, "Guide Globalization into a Just World Order," *TWQ* 24, No. 3 (Summer 2001); Simon Serfaty, "The New Normalcy," *TWQ* 25, No. 2 (Spring 2002); Michael J. Mazarr, "Saved from Ourselves?" *TWQ* 25, No. 2 (Spring 2002); Christopher Layne, "Offshore Balancing Revisited," *TWQ* 25, No. 2 (Spring 2002); Steven E. Miller, "The End of Unilateralism or Unilateralism Redux?" *TWQ* 25, No. 1 (Winter 2002).

Selection and introduction, copyright © 2002 by The Center for Strategic and International Studies and the Massachusetts Institute of Technology.

All rights reserved. No part of this book may be reproduced in any form or by any means, electronic or mechanical, including photocopying, recording, or by any information storage and retrieval system, without permission in writing from The MIT Press. For information, please address The MIT Press, Journals Department, Five Cambridge Center, Cambridge, MA 02142.

Library of Congress Cataloging-in-Publication Data

What does the world want from America? : international perspectives on U.S. foreign policy / edited by Alexander T.J. Lennon
    p.   cm. — (A Washington quarterly reader)
    Includes bibliographical references.
    ISBN 0-262-62167-3 (pbk. : alk. paper)
    1. United States—Foreign relations—2001– 2. United States—Foreign relations—Philosophy. 3. United States—Foreign public opinion. I. Lennon, Alexander T. II. Series.
    E902.T48 2002
    327.73'09'0511—dc21

                                                            2002026486

Library
University of Texas
at San Antonio

CONTENTS

Alexander T. J. Lennon

Introduction: Through the Looking Glass

Editorial pages and the halls of Washington are often filled with discussions about U.S. interests. Yet much of this discussion is introspective: What do we, as Americans, want from the world? What should we, in Washington, do around the world to secure those interests? And what do we, the United States, want the world to do? Such an introspective debate is appropriate to determine and pursue national interests and, as a government, to promote and defend the interests of its citizens, just as any other government would. To the extent that these debates ignore what the rest of the world wants, however, the United States risks losing the confidence, if not provoking the ire, of the rest of the world. The United States also may overlook opportunities to work with the rest of the world to pursue mutual goals and, where interests diverge, negotiate among conflicting ones.

This book stands those introspective questions on their heads. In essence, the chapters in Part I can be conceived as a mosaic of prescriptions, or reflections, for the United States. In that sense, they function as a looking glass that reflects on the United States, not other countries, as strategic thinkers from around the world answer the question, "In an ideal world, what role would you want the United States to perform with your country and region?" Admittedly, there is some fantasy in this exercise: no government will determine its interests based solely on the ad-

Alexander T. J. Lennon is editor-in-chief of *The Washington Quarterly* and is pursuing his Ph.D. in policy studies, part-time, at the University of Maryland's School of Public Affairs.

vice of those outside its borders. Yet that is what we hope makes the responses so interesting: the authors' unique perspectives on the role that the United States could perform in today's, and tomorrow's, world.

To attempt to answer these questions we began by soliciting responses from various regions of the globe. Although every country could not reasonably be represented, we believe the twelve articles included in Part I of this volume provide an appropriate sample of world opinion. It is critically important that the reader not misconstrue the authors' viewpoints as the national consensus of their respective countries. Just as a wide variety of assumptions, opinions, and recommendations exist among U.S. authors, each chapter is an individual's perception partially shaped by their national experiences and perspectives. They are not, however, national positions, nor should they be perceived as representing a national consensus.

In seeking authors, we made a conscious effort to avoid those who are, or hope to become, political leaders. Frankly, political figures may be constrained from expressing their individual thoughts and could in turn produce political statements. Most of the authors included here are preeminent figures in academia or think tanks. In many cases, they have spent some of their professional careers in the United States.

Our guidance consisted merely of a one-page invitation focusing on the question, "In an ideal world, what role would you want the United States to perform with your country and region?" We asked the authors not necessarily to refer to current U.S. policy but rather to use this opportunity to lay out an ideal world—even if it is a fantasy—where the United States plays the role that they wish to see. This intentionally left tremendous latitude for the authors, whose perspectives in Part I are presented roughly in order of those located geographically furthest from, to those nearest to, the United States.

With such latitude, some different perspectives, a number of common themes, and notable differences emerge. Although it is not fair to the authors to attempt to summarize their work, for fear of misrepresenting the nuances of their analysis and prescriptions, previewing these similarities and differences to help focus the reader's attention may be worthwhile.

First, no country, willingly or unwillingly, will arguably be involved as globally as the United States. While reading these prescriptions, one might consider the scope of each author's perspective—does each contemplate concerns globally, or is the focus regional, or even national?

Second, the degree to which each author relies on, or is ready to discard, the role of the nation-state in today's world is notable. What does globalization mean to, or even to what extent has it reached, each of these authors? Maria Claudia Drummond from Brazil, for example, focuses her chapter on the role that the United States could play globally. Others discuss local or national concerns.

Beyond these questions, a few common themes are worth mentioning to synergistically introduce the authors' work in Part I. The first and most obvious theme is that U.S. power is unparalleled. Although acknowledging the economic and military superiority of the United States, Peter Ludlow, based in Brussels, did question whether the size of the economic gap between the United States and the rest of the world is as big as rhetoric would have one believe and whether the gap in military power is really relevant in today's world. Nevertheless he, and just about every other author, acknowledged the U.S. economic and/or military lead in comparative national power.

Second, many authors expressed concern with the way Washington wields its power. No author explicitly declares that their country should seek to balance the United States or become its global peer because of their concerns. Some authors, such as Wu Xinbo from China and Pascal Boniface from France, even explicitly reject that idea. The only exception is arguably a vague warning by South African specialists Francis Kornegay, Chris Landsberg, and Steve McDonald that Africa should be taken "more seriously" or a "less benign 'G-8' of the South may be inevitable." In other words, as both Wu and Akio Watanabe from Japan argued, the key is not whether, but *how*, the United States should lead.

Some, such as Watanabe, simply highlight the potential dangers of complacency and arrogance that could naturally accompany a preponderance of power. Taken to their logical conclusion, these strategies risk evolving into isolationism or unilateralism. Others, such as Boniface, were more explicit in their criticism. Wu and Dmitri Trenin of Russia specifically criticized the United States for interfering in domestic political affairs of other countries. The degree of concern, and the tone in which it was expressed, varied widely. Most, such as Michael Stürmer from Germany and Drummond from Brazil, recommended a greater U.S. reliance on multilateralism. In contrast, Barry Rubin from Israel was the only author expressing no such concern.

A handful of authors expressed a third theme: a desire for U.S. military superiority to continue. Watanabe and Rubin explicitly stated this in their analysis, as well as Chong Guan Kwa and See Seng Tan in their co-authored chapter from Singapore. That is not to say that these authors unequivocally support U.S. military strength, however, as some of them express reservations about potential dangers derived from unilateralist concerns similar to those mentioned earlier.

A fourth, and potentially most surprising, theme emerged from at least three authors who independently highlighted that the same potential asset is being underutilized: U.S. science and technology. Wu, Mahmood Sariolghalam from Iran, and Kanti Bajpai from India all called for the United States to share its technological resources more liberally to help address issues of concern around the globe or at least with their particular country.

By highlighting these four common themes, I do not mean to imply that this comprehensively covers the similarities throughout these articles. Each reader will undoubtedly find their own threads of agreement, and disagreement, among different authors. This introduction simply is meant to serve as a starting point to provoke you, the reader, to draw your own lessons from this book.

One area of disagreement worth mentioning is the authors' varying prescriptions for the extent or manner of U.S. involvement in the world. Although no author recommended that the United States retreat to its own borders, some advocated deeper bilateral relations with their home country. Bajpai, for example, suggested five areas of cooperation for a deeper partnership with India. Others, such as Kornegay, Landsberg, and McDonald, recommended a different means of U.S. engagement, focusing on subregional and multilateral actors in Africa rather than just bilateral relations. Still others, such as Trenin, wanted "less" from the United States, although he strongly emphasized the importance of respect from Washington, a theme common to many other authors as well. Sariolghalam explained that if U.S. interaction in the world was based on fairness, rather than realpolitik, relations with countries like Iran could improve. Although the general theme advocating U.S. engagement ran throughout every one of the chapters, each author in Part I recommended a different form for that U.S. role with their country, in their region, or toward the world as a whole.

Part II presents responses from U.S. authors to the first twelve articles from around the globe in Part One. These U.S. authors wrote their chapters in the immediate aftermath of the September 11 terrorist attacks. Although the authors do not necessarily argue that those terrorist attacks were inevitable because of U.S. global predominance, all four of them seek to find a balance between a U.S. role that provokes international hostility, from either states or transnational actors, and one that secures U.S. interests. From Steven E. Miller's skepticism that U.S. unilateralism will vanish to Simon Serfaty's depiction of the new normalcy of global strategic affairs, these authors looked at how the heightened awareness of the terrorist threat would or would not change the U.S. role in the world. Coupled with Christopher Layne's prescription for offshore balancing and Michael J. Mazarr's appeal to capitalize on a post–September 11 window of global sympathy, all the authors give their view of how the U.S. role in the world may, or should, change in the coming years in light of global perceptions of the United States.

The articles in this volume intend to provide global perspectives and a starting point for debates about benevolent leadership, perceptions of U.S. hegemony, and ultimately the potential rise and fall of great powers. How long can a superpower remain a superpower if it does not seek the same goals as the rest of the world? How similar must those goals be? The first question to ask is: How similar are those goals now? This book explores that preliminary question.

Our goal in this book is to stimulate you, as a reader, to learn from the authors' insight, challenge their thoughts, and continue the debates yourselves (whether in a classroom, online, in the halls of power, or elsewhere). With due recognition to Lewis Caroll, you can begin by enjoying Wonderland in the first part of this book, where U.S. policy is prescribed from abroad. You might be surprised by what you find when you enter the looking glass....

Part I: How the World Sees the United States

Wu Xinbo

To Be an Enlightened Superpower

The twentieth century passed with a vivid U.S. fingerprint on almost every aspect of human life. As we move into the twenty-first century, the magic of globalization and the information age has rendered U.S. influence omnipresent on the earth. The United States' primary role in world affairs is understood, but for many observers, it is full of contradictions. The United States pledges to stand for human rights and democracy, but this promise is coupled with a certain degree of hypocrisy. The United States claims to promote peace and stability but often intrudes into the internal affairs of others by abusing its supreme military power or waving the stick of sanctions. The United States cherishes a high degree of self-pride but often neglects to show respect to, and consideration for, the national feelings of others. Washington tends to seek absolute security for itself but is inclined to dismiss the legitimate security concerns of other countries.

Without the United States the world might be less stable and prosperous; but Washington certainly can do better in promoting peace, harmony, and prosperity in the world. Hypothetically, how can the United States act as an enlightened superpower? In particular, from a Chinese perspective, what are the ideal policies the United States should under-

Wu Xinbo is a professor at the Center for American Studies at Fudan University in China.

Copyright © 2001 by The Center for Strategic and International Studies and the Massachusetts Institute of Technology
The Washington Quarterly • 24:3 pp . 63–71.

take in dealing with China and the Asia–Pacific region? To explore what an ideal U.S. policy should look like, the baseline must necessarily be current U.S. policy.

Neither Rosy nor Grimy Glasses

An ideal U.S. policy toward China should be based on a correct perception of China. The United States should develop a full appreciation of three issues before a sound China policy can be developed: how to understand progress and problems in a fast-changing China, how to treat a rising China with respect, and how to define the nature of Sino–U.S. relations.

The Chinese have always been upset by an oversimplified U.S. view of China. From 1979 to the spring of 1989, the United States had viewed China through rose-colored glasses. In that light, China was a country embracing economic reform, political liberalization, and a diversified social life. After the Tiananmen Square conflict, the United States swung to the other extreme, looking at China through a grimy lens and seeing a country that violates human rights, restricts religious freedom, pollutes the environment, and bullies Taiwan.

In fact, understanding China has never been that simple. China has made huge progress over the past two decades toward turning itself into a modern country. At the same time, it has been carrying too much historical baggage and now faces many new challenges. China is not as good as U.S. observers used to believe in the 1980s, but it is not as bad as they assume in the post-Tiananmen period.

In the real world, the Americans, affected by their cultural background, may never be able to overcome a black-and-white approach to understanding China. In an ideal world, policymakers in Washington would take a more balanced view of China's achievements and problems and be reasonably patient when expecting more fundamental and positive changes in this country. Moreover, U.S. policy would be geared to facilitate China's progress, not to hamper it. For example, on the issue of human rights, the United States should welcome China's progress, while acknowledging the complexity of this issue and help China develop its social, economic, and political conditions to improve human rights even further. U.S. human rights policy should not be focused on sponsoring anti-China bills at the annual Geneva conference of the United Nations Human Rights Commission and on supporting a handful of political dissidents.

A second problem is the U.S. attitude toward a rising China. In the 1980s, the U.S. political elite stated that a strong China would help promote regional stability and serve U.S. interests. At the time, they perceived that a more powerful China would contribute to U.S. efforts to contain the Soviet Union. With the end of the Cold War, U.S. policymakers no longer publicly claimed that they would like to see the emergence of a strong China. Instead, many U.S. strategists expressed concern, either publicly or privately, over the "China threat." Absent a strategic necessity to play the China card against a more threatening power, some U.S. policymakers worry that a stronger China would undermine the paramount U.S. position in East Asia and pose a challenge to U.S. interests in the region. In the real world, such a selfish and parochial view does have its currency; in an ideal world, however, the U.S. political elite would put China's rise in a broad perspective. First and foremost, they would come to realize that a stronger China will benefit the Chinese people. Having suffered from poverty and weakness in their modern history, the Chinese are eager to make their country wealthy and strong, and there is nothing wrong with their genuine wishes to reach this goal.

Moreover, a strong China would promote regional stability. The past has shown that, when China was poor and weak, a power vacuum emerged in the East Asia region. Chaos and turmoil prevailed in the midst of various powers' efforts to build their spheres of influence. Contrary to the concern of those who perceive a "China threat," a strong China is unlikely to be detrimental to regional stability. As Ambassador Chas W. Freeman convincingly argued, "China is not Germany, Japan, the USSR, or even the United States. China does not seek lebensraum; is not pursuing its manifest destiny; does not want to incorporate additional non-

Han peoples into its territory; has no ideology to export; and is certainly not a colonizer and does not station any troops overseas."[1]

Most importantly, the reemergence of China as a major power coincides with China's integration into the world community, which means that, as China accumulates greater material strength, it is also learning to become a responsible power. The past two decades have shown that China has become more responsive to, and cooperative with, international society. Based on this understanding, first, the United States should view the rise of China as an inevitable trend, welcome it, and interpret it as a great opportunity for peace and prosperity. Second, it should facilitate rather than obstruct China's growth into a world power and be sympathetic to China's pursuit of its legitimate national interests. Third, the United States should, through its own conduct, provide China with a model of behavior as a responsible power in the international community.

The third issue is the U.S. understanding of its relations with China. Two assumptions tend to complicate Sino–U.S. ties: that China and the United States have no common values and therefore cannot develop intimate relations; and that U.S. relations with China should be second to U.S. relations with historical allies in the region, such as Japan, South Korea, and Australia. The first assumption is flawed because, in fact, common interests do exist between these two countries. Although differing in ideology and political system, China and the United States have a wide range of common interests at the global, regional, and bilateral levels. History demonstrates that ideology has not impeded Sino–U.S. cooperation on many important issues that serve mutual interests. In international relations, what matters is not a country's ideology and political system, but its external behavior.

The second assumption is fallacious because it overlooks the fact that China is geopolitically more influential than any of the three U.S. allies in the region: Japan, the Republic of Korea, or Australia. For peace and stability in Northeast Asia, Southeast Asia, South Asia, or Central Asia, Beijing can play a more important role than Tokyo, Seoul, or Canberra. As China's economic boom grows, so will its weight in regional economic affairs, as demonstrated by its performance in the Asian financial crisis in 1997–1998. By refraining from devaluing its currency in the midst of the crisis, China helped prevent the already deteriorating regional economies from worsening.

In an ideal world, both the liberal and conservative wings of the U.S. political elite would judge the China–U.S. relationship on its own merits, not by political or security ideology. Washington would not predetermine China as either a "strategic partner" or "strategic competitor" but would define it through comprehensive interaction with Beijing. Although it would be prepared to handle ups and downs in bilateral relations, the United States would seek a better future for one of the most important relationships in the world. Finally, the U.S. political elite in the ideal world would prioritize statesmanship over domestic political disputes in relations with China, thus ameliorating the environment in which to develop Sino–U.S. ties.

The Taiwan Question

Questions surrounding two crucial policy issues—Taiwan and Asia–Pacific regional security—will determine the future of Sino–U.S. ties.[2] The Taiwan question is the crux of U.S.–China security problems. It is probably the only issue that may ignite a major military conflict between China and the United States and completely destroy bilateral ties.

In general, the Chinese hold three assumptions about U.S. policy toward Taiwan. Strategically, China believes the United States still views Taiwan as part of its "sphere of influence" in the western Pacific, a quasi-ally in the region. Politically, China believes the United States favors Taiwan's independence. Although the United States does not want to fight for Taiwan's independence, it prefers the maintenance of the status quo, namely, the de facto independence of Taiwan. Militarily, China believes the United States will continue to provide Taiwan with assistance, including the transfer of advanced arms and military technology, intelligence, and training. Should China resort to the use of force to integrate Taiwan, the United States would certainly intervene.

Those assumptions, true or not, reflect the mainstream Chinese inter-pretation of U.S.–Taiwan policy.

Ideally, the United States would think differently about the Taiwan headache and view the problem basically as a matter of nation-building for China, not as a U.S. issue in either a geopolitical or ideological sense. The United States would also understand that, in the long run, for Taiwan to gain security, international space, and greater economic opportunities, it must accept some association with the mainland while preserving its utmost political autonomy. If Taiwan seeks formal inde-pendence, Beijing will almost certainly resort to the use of force. If those events come to pass, even if China is not able to take over Tai-wan, it certainly is able to throw the island into chaos.

Should the United States intervene at that point, it will have to make an extremely difficult decision about what price it is willing to pay to maintain, at a minimum, the present situation on Taiwan. U.S. military involvement, which would create even more trouble in the Tai-wan Strait, will not end the problem. Compared with such a horrible scenario, peaceful reunification is in the best interests of Beijing, Taipei, and Washington.

Most importantly, U.S. policymakers would realize that, as long as the current U.S. Taiwan policy continues, Washington can never place its re-lations with a rising power on a solid basis. Beijing will remain suspicious of, and concerned about, the U.S. security presence in East Asia. The U.S. leadership would also not be able to expect Beijing's endorsement on strategic initiatives in regional and global affairs. Should the Taiwan issue be resolved peacefully, however, China will become a status quo power in the political–security sense; Sino–U.S. relations will be far more stable, healthy, and constructive; and China–U.S. cooperation will stand as a strong force for regional security and prosperity.

Based on this wisdom, an ideal U.S. Taiwan policy would adopt a re-freshing new outlook. First, Washington would reorient its goal on the Taiwan issue from a "peaceful solution" to "peaceful reunification," be-cause "peaceful solution" implies two possibilities: Taiwan's peaceful in-dependence or peaceful reunification with China. By unequivocally pledging to support China's peaceful reunification with Taiwan, the United States would dismiss the ambiguity in, and Chinese suspicion of, its Taiwan policy. Only by so doing can there be a peaceful solution for the disputes across the Taiwan Strait. Second, Washington would encourage Taipei to negotiate a reasonable arrangement for reunification with Beijing. Washington can act as an honest broker by presenting useful and creative ideas about reconciliation across the Taiwan Strait, or it can exert pressure from behind the scenes on both sides when dilemmas stall the negotiations. If Taipei tries to push the envelope and provoke China, the United States would ideally stop it.

On the issue of arms sales to Taiwan, in an ideal world, the United States would adopt a more sensible and responsible approach. Washington would ardently honor its commitment to China in the 1982 Communiqué not to carry out a long-term policy of arms sales to Taiwan and gradually to reduce its arms sales to Taiwan, leading, over a period of time, to a final resolution.[3] Also, Washington would make its arms sale policy compatible with the ultimate goal of Taiwan's peaceful reunification with China.

Regional Issues

On the issue of regional security, several questions will test U.S. policymakers: how to restructure the U.S. military presence in the western Pacific in a changing security context; how to manage its security alliances in a new geopolitical setting; how to encourage Japan to play a larger role in regional security without upsetting existing balances; and, finally, how to deal with the issue of theater missile defense (TMD) in East Asia.

In an ideal world, the United States would no longer view its military presence in the western Pacific as a means of bolstering its strategic interests in the region. With the ongoing reconciliation and inevitable reunification of the Korean Peninsula and the resumption of a normal regional security role for Japan, the United Sates would understand that a large-scale, permanent military presence would not be politically sustainable either domestically or internationally. Ideally, as the international environment changes, Washington will try to find new ways to preserve its influence. For instance, a base-access arrangement in the region for U.S. forces would be more feasible politically and less expensive financially than maintaining a permanent presence in East Asia. The revolution in military affairs and the improvement of rapid-reaction capability will negate the need for the United States to keep a large armed force on foreign soil. Most importantly, Washington policymakers would understand that, in a time of growing economic interdependence and deepening regional integration, it is more relevant for the United States to lead by shaping the rules of the game and building a security community than to seek influence by showing off its military muscle.

Building security communities also affects the role of U.S. security alliances in the region. Washington's redefinition of its security alliance with Japan and others has clearly alarmed and alienated states such as China that have become very suspicious of U.S. strategic intentions. As countries feel threatened, they naturally respond by aligning with each other. The Chinese–Russian partnership, although still far from being an alliance, has become more substantive over the past several years in response to perceived aggressiveness by the United States in Asia and Europe. As a result, at a time when members in the Asia–Pacific region are supposed to build a community that promotes the security of all the regional members, U.S. reliance on alliances is deepening regional divisions.

In an ideal world, the United States would seek to promote common security (security for all), not unilateral security or collective security (security for some countries at the expense of others). In this context, Washington will play down the importance of security alliances. For existing alliances, the United States would stress their political rather than their military function and would seek closer diplomatic consultation and coordination among allies in dealing with regional issues, abstaining from rattling the alliance saber against a third party. Most importantly, policymakers in Washington would realize that a sound trilateral relationship among China, Japan, and the United States is crucial to peace and stability in the Asia–Pacific region. Therefore, instead of uniting with Japan against China, Washington would spare no efforts to promote constructive interactions among the three parties.

The notion of a "pluralistic security community" would ideally prevail in U.S. security ideology. Like an Asia–Pacific economic community that benefits all economies in the region, a security community would advance equal security for all regional members. As Admiral Dennis Blair argues, "[S]ecurity communities are the right way ahead for the Asia–Pacific region." According to him, the goal is to build upon the current set of principally bilateral security relationships in the Asia–Pacific region to form a web of partnerships leading to mature security communities.[4] In this context, "pluralistic" means that the community is not based on a single pillar, but on several variables such as the consensus of major powers, the role of security alliances, regional or subregional mechanisms, and so forth. Differences in ideology and political systems should not obstruct cooperation on security issues. The United States would still play a significant role—not as a hegemonist, but as a key player.

In both the real and ideal worlds, Japan inevitably features prominently in U.S. policy configurations. The redefinition of the U.S.–Japan alliance, coupled with the rise of conservative political influence and nationalism in Japan as well as the perceived shift in Japan's security environment, has been driving Japan to become a traditional political–military power. An ideal U.S. policy toward Japan, however, would encourage Japan to remain a civilian and pacifist country. Realizing that Japan will and should become a normal state, the United States would advise Japan to be serious and responsible in dealing with its World War II legacy and to be sensitive to its Asian neighbors' concerns about Japan's future behavior. Although expecting Japan to play a larger and more active role in regional affairs, Washington would avoid pushing Japan to assume a high profile on security issues and to expand its already impressive military capability. With regard to the revision of Japan's Peace Constitution—particularly Article IX—Washington would urge Tokyo to take into account the possible negative impact of such an action on regional stability as well as Japan's future. The U.S. administration would advise Japan's political elite to be cautious and responsible in dealing with one of the most important political legacies of modern Japan.

In an ideal world, Washington would not be addicted to the idea of deploying TMD in East Asia because it would understand the high risk of altering the existing strategic stability in the region and inviting an arms race. Even though security challenges to U.S. interests in the region will still exist, as a responsible power, the United States would be inclined to respond to such challenges mainly through nonmilitary means. For instance, Washington would seek to improve political relations with regional members, encourage economic cooperation and regional integration, develop a security community, and promote arms control measures. U.S. policymakers would firmly believe that U.S. security interests and regional stability were best preserved through arms reduction, not arms buildup.

Beyond Hegemony

Economic factors have become the most powerful engine for China–U.S. relations. The development of economic ties, however, has been invariably constrained by the conservative attitude of the United States on technology transfers and the politicization of economic issues. In both bilateral and multilateral settings, Washington has been pushing the agenda for trade and investment liberalization while neglecting the call from developing economies for bolder technology transfer on the part of developed countries. In particular, the United States maintains a discriminatory technology transfer policy toward China on the pretext of national security. The U.S. debate over whether to give China permanent normal trade relations and to facilitate its World Trade Organization membership was an example of efforts to politicize economic relations.

In a best-case scenario, however, the United States would consider the advanced science and technology it has developed as a public good it can provide to all countries. While benefiting from such technology, those countries would work cooperatively and wholeheartedly to build world peace in return. In other words, advanced science and technology would no longer be a monopoly of the developed countries, but a means to promote peace, harmony, and prosperity on earth. Moreover, economic relations would not be affected by political considerations.

The twentieth century has often been characterized as the "American Century." In the twenty-first century, like it or not, the United States will continue to play a leading role in the world. The question for the United States and others is not whether it should play a role in world affairs, but how it should play this role. In reality, Washington may never see the world from this perspective, but the United States certainly will want to be a benign superpower, as some Americans often claim. To achieve that goal, Washington should not be content with the way it has been doing business. It should keep learning about the perspective of others, thus serving the interests of the United States and the rest of the world as well.

Notes

1. Chas W. Freeman Jr., "An Interest-Based China Policy" in Hans Binnendijk and Ronald N. Montaperto, eds., *Strategic Trends in China* (Washington, D.C.: National Defense University Press, 1998), 123–124.

2. Wu Xinbo, "U.S. Security Policy in Asia: Implications for China–U.S. Relations" *Contemporary Southeast Asia* 22 (December 2000): 3.

3. "United States–China Joint Communiqué on United States Arms Sales to Taiwan" in Harry Harding, *A Fragile Relationship: The United States and China Since 1972* (Washington, D.C.: The Brookings Institution), 383–385.

4. Dennis C. Blair and John T. Hanley Jr., "From Wheels to Webs: Reconstructing Asia–Pacific Security Arrangements," *Washington Quarterly* 24, no. 1 (Winter 2001).

Akio Watanabe

First among Equals

Fundamentally, Japan shares a wide range of values and interests with the United States. The essentially similar long-term goals of these two nations, whose economies produce nearly 43 percent of the world's wealth, facilitate envisioning a world order that would be ideal from both countries' viewpoints. Such a world order would be premised on democracy, human rights, and free markets. Based on these principles, Japan would willingly support this world order. In fact, the United States, as the ultimate guarantor of such an order, is unlikely to meet substantive objections from any of the major players on the world stage. Nevertheless, while promoting this world order, the United States must be cautious and attentive to local conditions around the world.

For this ideal situation to be realized—at least with regard to Asia— two requirements must be met: a continued working partnership between the United States and Japan and a solid base of public support for the domestic and international goals of both nations.

A Matter of Perspective

The great challenge for the United States in securing this ideal world order will be coming to terms with its unprecedented relative and abso-

Akio Watanabe is professor emeritus of the University of Tokyo and president of the Research Institute for Peace and Security in Tokyo, Japan.

Copyright © 2001 by The Center for Strategic and International Studies and the Massachusetts Institute of Technology
The Washington Quarterly • 24:3 pp. 73–81.

lute power. Already evident are two diametrically opposed risks: complacency and arrogance.

As with Gulliver on his travels, it is all a matter of perspective. The self-complacent protagonist may easily shirk his global responsibilities. Yielding to self-absorption, indifference, or just plain laziness, he may not even realize how gossamer-thin is the tissue of multilateral obligations that enmeshes him with the smaller and weaker members of the international community. For example, the United States may not heed what global warming means to the Lilliputian island nation of Micronesia. Naturally, for them, any portent of the Pacific Ocean's waves swamping their islands is of the utmost concern.

By the same token, the din of humanitarian disasters in faraway places with unpronounceable names is unlikely to motivate a self-complacent United States, unless others can somehow demonstrate that responding to them complements Washington's immediate self-interest. In either of these cases, other countries will be highly attuned to any sign that the United States is preparing to neglect or abandon them.

Conversely, Gulliver may become all too conscious of his own real or imaginary weaknesses and shortcomings; he may fall prey to suspicion, doubt, anxiety, and fear of the unknown. This paranoid protagonist will meddle in everyone else's business on the spur of the moment, foisting his own preferences on others with scant regard to the actual needs of the people and the regions concerned—all, ostensibly, in the name of "moral leadership." The danger here is overreaction to perceived crises—humanitarian or otherwise—under pressure of domestic public opinion agitated by CNN.

U.S. unilateralism is thus simply the other side of the coin from U.S. isolationism. From the perspective of the smaller members of the international community, the sheer unpredictability of the superpower's behavior is most disturbing. Irrational swings between isolationism and internationalism, between complacency and arrogance, are part and parcel of an unfortunately recurring pattern in U.S. history—a story as old as the United States itself.

New in the twenty-first century, however, are the repercussions these swings will have on international events, simply because of the sheer disproportion of U.S. power. Whether as formal allies or as potential antagonists, all nations in the world expect certain things of the United States, just as if they were its clients. They watchfully anticipate every U.S. move, lest they be abandoned, trampled, or entangled—the typical attitude of the junior party of an alliance toward its superior. Now more than ever, what the United States does is just as important as what it does not do.

When trying to understand the U.S. point of view and craft appropriate responses, Asians must keep the U.S. perspective in mind. Ironically, the prize for being the sole superpower is, by definition, that one is surrounded by potential antagonists, resulting in extreme sensitivity to any sign of external threats coupled with an obsession for absolute security. The quest to build a Fortress America—impregnably armed with a national defense missile system—is clearly part of this superpower syndrome.

The United States must therefore learn to be highly cautious in discharging its global responsibility. As the sole superpower, with global reach in both soft and hard power, the United States would be wise never to lose sight of the unique international role it plays. Above all, it should prudently adopt an attentive, watchful, and flexible stance, in order to remain sensitive to local conditions.

Commonly, nations—no less than individuals—will profess the same values in an abstract sense, but will rarely agree in actual practice on how those values should be implemented. The concept of human rights, for example, for any given country is substantively grounded in the tangible effects of legal procedure. Ultimately, however, the energy behind the concept emanates from intangibles, probing into the very question, "What is humanity?" The answer of course will differ broadly from culture to culture and civilization to civilization. Even a cursory review of the concepts of democracy and market economies reveals that they are nebulous, meaning different things to different people; indeed, at different times, they may even mean different things to the same people. Both a problem and an opportunity result: as a practical matter, the abstract concepts of human rights, democracy, and free markets are easily turned into slogans, which can be used as much to unite as to divide people. When grounded in the concrete reality of practical politics, they become the policies that make or unmake our strategic relationships.

For example, a group of Western nations (led by the United States) has been critical of non-Western (and especially Asian) countries' reported violations of human rights. Despite the compromise reached at the World Conference on Human Rights in Vienna in June 1993, the gap between the Western emphasis on civil and political rights and the Asian preference for economic, social, and cultural rights remains. The financial typhoon that hit many Asian countries in 1997 further exposed these discrepancies. Many Western commentators declared that the financial crises demonstrated the failure of Asian "developmental capitalism" in face of a superior, Western model. Little doubt exists that authoritarian regimes or dictatorships, and their attendant economic models (sometimes called "crony capitalism"), are things of the past. Yet many experts on the Asian economy believe that mechanistically applying the so-called IMF (International Monetary Fund) model will not provide an ideal solution.

The search for a new model continues. As this process unfolds, the United States must remember that Asia's ongoing reforms will not necessarily lead to U.S.-style capitalism or democracy. The free market, regardless of its theoretical excellence as an economic model, cannot function smoothly in practice unless it rises as a function of each society's indigenous conditions. The same setting holds true for democracy. One cannot simply "import" democracy from abroad by writing constitutions and holding elections.

In this new and ideal world order, therefore, as allies and friends, we should most appropriately speak of "democracies and market economies" in the plural. Pluralism is indeed a key term here, referring simply to the existence of diversity. Tolerance of diversity does not necessarily need to mean the same thing as endorsement of relativism. An ideal world order would include various types of democratic states living together and various forms of market economies flourishing side by side.

Above all, the ideal world order would not be uniform. Indeed, if everything were ultimately measured in terms of economic efficiency, a horrific type of "one world-ism" would prevail. Global standards are good for enhancing instrumental values (such as entrepreneurial dynamism) but are not necessarily beneficial for the sake of intrinsic values (such as spiritual serenity). If the eventual outcome of a free-trade world is the victory of uniformity, undoubtedly the result would be an ironic defeat for democracy. Hopefully, that world does not wait for us in the new century.

The Imperative of Collective Action

Such an ideal world will not be free from conflict among states. Keeping the peace, however, will be much easier if the military preeminence of the United States lasts for the foreseeable future. This preeminence is a stabilizing element because, as a general rule, unbridgeable gaps in the military capabilities of countries make war between them unlikely in the modern age. Risks would outweigh the gains of potential success, and a weaker country or group of countries would not dare of its own accord challenge stronger ones, unless highly provoked. A second Pearl Harbor can be safely ruled out in the foreseeable future.

Apart from such comprehensive, global considerations, many regional problems can be solved or, at any rate, ameliorated only through continued engagement and collegial action between allies, based on the principles outlined above. As a result, to obtain the results it desires from coordinated action, the United States must expect, and be prepared for, all sorts of time- and energy-consuming demands as the world's security manager. As the experiences of the North Atlantic Treaty Organization (NATO) or the U.S.–Japan alliance amply demonstrate, despite all the good will in the world, hammering out a workable formula for power sharing and the division of labor is not easy. Even when that task can be accomplished, one must then sell the resulting arrangements to the public.

As the proverb goes, too many cooks spoil the broth. Political leadership, more than military leadership, is subject to local sentiment and parochial perspective. Certainly, in war, each new level of command raises, by degrees, the potential for confusion. Furthermore, because the stakes are lower, collaboration during peacetime is far more difficult than in times of war or crisis. Politics is neither cookery nor war; for most issues, precisely collective or collegial leadership is needed. Except in extreme situations, dividing leadership among colleagues, not dictating it from one place, is the best option.

Asian Regional Perspective

The Asia–Pacific region displays both reassuring and disconcerting trends. Overall, the news is good. Not much imagination is required to grasp the tremendous progress that many nations in this region have made during the last century. One hundred years ago—a mere bump in the region's long march through history—colonial Western powers ruled the greater part of Southeast Asia, except for Thailand. The immemorial Chinese Empire was in creeping decline, yielding to the encroachments of Western imperialism. Japan was preparing to absorb Korea. The Commonwealth of Australia was in its infancy.

Only since World War II and the end of colonialism can one truly speak of the emergence of a genuine regional system of international relations in Asia and the Pacific. Indeed, just a few decades have passed since the two largest European settlements of the South Pacific (Australia and New Zealand) gained their political independence. Despite occasional setbacks, in this part of the world today, we witness a youthful, vibrant, growing group of nation-states. This dynamism is a distinctive feature of Asia, in contrast to other regions of the developing world.

Some disquieting phenomena, however, move hand in hand with these reassuring trends. Despite progress, the region remains undoubtedly the world's most explosive; the two major hot wars of the Cold War were fought in Asia. Moreover, nation building, a central project of post-colonial development, remains an unfinished business in Asia:

witness the continuing division of Korea and the undetermined status of Taiwan. Other Southeast Asian states (Myanmar, Vietnam, Indonesia, the Philippines, and Malaysia) are not yet firmly consolidated. Their frailty was exposed during the 1990s, when they were caught in the rising tide of globalization, with its attendant ups and downs.

Such signs warrant caution, but should not lead to the conclusion that Asia's twenty-first century prospects are dim. On the contrary, the future appears bright and encouraging. Ongoing political turmoil and confusion might well amount to nothing more than the growing pains of youthful states, rather than a congenital condition. Little likelihood exists that Asia will stagnate or fall to the fringe of the international community.

Thus, for the United States to rearrange its foreign policy orientation away from Asia, for whatever reason, would be absurd. Doing so would be a blunder from every point of view: a self-inflicted wound of world-shaking magnitude. Undoubtedly, the United States is currently absorbed in the process of building momentum toward economic integration of the Western Hemisphere, and this process will accelerate through instruments such as the North American Free Trade Agreement (NAFTA). Yet the United States must not lose sight of opportunities to play a constructive role in Asian regional organizations, such as the APEC (Asia–Pacific Economic Cooperation) forum or the ASEAN Regional Forum (ARF).

By the same token, the United States should adopt a more relaxed attitude toward the "Asianization" of Asia. In the past, the United States tended to be hypersensitive to any idea of regional cooperation in Asia, simply because the United States was not considered a constituting member, whether of Malaysia's plan for the EAEC (East Asian Economic Caucus) or Japan's proposal for an AMF (Asian Monetary Fund). This "Asianization" process, which in principle is highly desirable, is part of the price the United States must pay for perceived U.S. aloofness during the Asian financial crisis of 1997. Partially because of this experience, some Asian countries recently began to investigate the possibility of bilateral free-trade arrangements. For example, in January

2001, Japan and Singapore concluded an Economic Agreement for a New Age Partnership.

The Great Enigma: China

Despite these other challenges, the region's most daunting challenge is presented by its largest member—not because China, like the Soviet Union in the past, poses an actual military threat, although indeed it potentially is; but rather because it is an enigma on so many fronts. Apart from their vast population and territory, the Chinese are justly proud of the fact that they had attained a high-level civilization when Rome was nothing but seven wild hills overrun by wolves. China has long been the center of a magnificent world all its own.

Despite this vantage, or rather because of it, the Celestial Empire failed to adapt to modernity and was forced to endure the humiliation of serving as a quasi-colonial nation for about 100 years beginning in the mid-nineteenth century. After a long period of national tribulation, China is now at last on the verge of becoming a genuinely sovereign state.

With its newly acquired economic power, China ardently seeking "equal" standing among the advanced powers of the world is no small wonder. In the eighteenth or nineteenth centuries, when a classic paradigm of realpolitik prevailed in international relations, this accession would have been a matter of course. Contemporary international society is, however, substantially different now. All nations, small and large, are closely intertwined in a complex web of interdependence. The global village is a reality, and it has no room for what Kenneth Boulding has called "unconditional viability," either in the economic or the strategic sphere. Without mutual tolerance, forbearance, and compromise, none of us will survive, let alone flourish.

China should be allowed to take its rightful place in the sun. We may well be excused for holding back on other emerging nations (such as India), but foreseeing the problems of acting otherwise toward China requires no stretch of the imagination. Under the existing principle of national sovereignty, each state's leaders are primarily responsible for providing for their population's economic and social welfare. Everyone, including China's leaders, realizes that the Chinese cannot expect to solve their economic problems unilaterally.

The consequences of China's economic modernization will be enormous. Simply in terms of the physical world in which we live, if modernization continues to be successful and maintains its current pace, it will place a huge burden on the environment. For example, try forecasting, with China in the mix, a future equilibrium of demand and supply of natural resources such as oil and gas. Conversely, if China's economic modernization fares poorly, social dislocation on an unprecedented scale and political upheavals are not unfathomable. Either through success or through failure, or—as is more likely—something in between, China's future is destined to affect the life of every human being in the twenty-first century.

Although differences between past and present are evident, the lessons of history are well worth examination; they provide insight into how things may turn out and what must be done to ensure a positive outcome. In some ways, the Chinese problem resembles the German problem or the Japanese problem that vexed neighboring countries when each quickly emerged as great powers. Regardless of their underlying intentions, the mere emergence of Germany and Japan necessarily aroused the concern of the existing great powers. Following unification in the late nineteenth century, and well into the twentieth, Germany experienced fierce economic friction with its advanced neighbors, especially Great Britain. Japan had a similar experience with the colonial powers in Asia during the 1930s. Japan's economic competition with the United States during the 1970s and 1980s was intense, but could only be characterized as benign.

Economic competition thus does not have to be a precursor to military strife. Yet it takes great effort to prevent economic disputes from spilling into other unexpected and sometimes malignant rivalries. Indeed, recently the West suspiciously viewed Japan as a power comprised of elements ultimately incompatible with Western ideals and essentially "not like us."

China will likely face a similar ordeal. For the time being, by virtue of being a fast-rising power, China poses perplexing questions to its neighboring countries and to the prospective new world order. Given China's deeply ingrained sense of frustration, attributable to unpleasant memories of its recent past, it will probably continue to voice its international concerns in revolutionary language, and perhaps even behave belligerently to some extent. The United States must possess and utilize a far-ranging insight into Asian psychology and, above all, great patience and forbearance to respond in a manner allowing itself to accomplish its objectives and help us all build that bright new world order.

An Ideal Division of Labor

As stated at the outset, little disagreement between Japan and the United States about what should be done in an ideal new world order exists. Disagreements that may arise will more likely be about how things should be done.

Japan's continuing inclination to address the "soft" elements of a comprehensive security strategy, while leaving the "hard" elements to the United States, is one harbinger of how this pattern of behavior might ultimately translate into a division of labor. Nevertheless, even if Japan departs from its unique view of collective self-defense—namely, that it has the right to participate in collective self-defense but chooses not to exercise that right—the Japanese military's extraregional role in international affairs will continue to be modest. On the other hand, Japan's military contribution to the security of the region, as a powerful, well-equipped, and steady U.S. ally, will remain an important part of the security equation. The U.S. Forces in Japan (USFJ) should start thinking of the Japan Self-Defense Forces (JSDF) as a colleague. Japan will remain an auxiliary to the United States, not just because of the "peace constitution," but because of the simple reality of the enormous gap in military capabilities between Japan and the United States. In any case, the Japanese concept of comprehensive security is based on the application of economic and nonviolent measures. Japan's fondness for that concept is related to a general Japanese cultural preference for the indirect approach.

The success of any U.S. economic or security strategy in Asia—particularly with regard to engagement with China—ultimately depends on a firm bond of friendship between Japan and the United States. First, in terms of cultural issues, Japan plays a valuable role as an interpreter of "the Asian mind." Second, despite the bizarre tragicomedy of Tokyo's efforts to deal with the country's economic malaise, Japan's influence will continue to be decisive in the region's economic development. Third, in terms of security issues, even in the age of "real time" and information technology, the enormous physical distance between the United States and East Asia is a serious drag on the projection of military force during a crisis. The forward deployment of U.S. forces in the vicinity of Japan will remain indispensable. In all these ways, Japan can help the United States enforce their common vision for democratic world order.

Kanti Bajpai

Add Five 'E's to Make a Partnership

The United States, ideally, should lay the groundwork for an endur-ing partnership with India, even though India has not been a high pri-ority in U.S. grand strategy. In the decade to come, however, Washington should build bridges to this awakening democratic giant. India's economy has never grown faster; its democracy remains vibrant, if noisy; its popu-lation, although growing at a slower rate, will surpass China's number and level off at 1.5 billion in the next half-century. Unlike other coun-tries, India is receptive to a deeper relationship with the sole super-power. A liberalized economy, a more internationalist attitude toward world politics, and an unprecedented appreciation of U.S. purposes and power are propelling India toward the United States.

An Indian–U.S. partnership would be a force for stability in world politics. Global stability will depend on peace and cooperation in Asia and a growing net of constructive interactions among the major pow-ers of this superregion. The United States is the linchpin here. India, on the other hand, is an emerging power with capabilities that extend to the Asia–Pacific region. Both countries have vital interests in Asia, from the Persian Gulf to East Asia and throughout the Indian Ocean. These common interests relate to oil supplies, proliferation, ethnic

Kanti Bajpai teaches at the School of International Studies at Jawaharlal Nehru University in New Delhi.

Copyright © 2001 by The Center for Strategic and International Studies and the Massachusetts Institute of Technology
The Washington Quarterly • 24:3 pp. 83–94.

disaffection, fundamentalism, terrorism, narcotics trafficking, freedom of the seas, safety of sea lanes, peaceful resolution of territorial disputes, and a balance of power. A full-fledged strategic partnership between the United States and India, however, is some time away. In the interim, New Delhi and Washington must build understanding, links, and a foundation of military and nonmilitary cooperation that will move them toward deeper engagement. As the more powerful country, the United States, ideally, would initiate this more thoroughgoing relationship.

Over the last few years, the United States has created the basis for a long-term partnership between the two countries. President Bill Clinton's visit to India in March 2000 and the Indian prime minister's return visit to the United States in September dramatized the new relationship. The Bush administration has the opportunity in five issue areas to go beyond mere visits: a strategic *entente*; *economics*; *energy*; *ecology*; and *epidemics*. The "vision statement" signed in New Delhi in March 2000 and affirmed in September conceives of an architecture built largely around these five "E"s.[1] The United States should now boldly do what no administration has done previously with India and put real bricks and mortar into the relationship.

Entente

At the heart of the partnership with India should be a strategic entente. During the next four years, the United States should cooperate with India to reduce global nuclear dangers; assist in Indian defense modernization; bring Pakistan and Kashmiri separatists to the negotiating table with New Delhi; work with Indian leaders to create a cooperative security system in Asia, like the Organization for Security and Cooperation in Europe (OSCE); and support India's bid for permanent membership on the United Nations (UN) Security Council.

Nuclear proliferation has historically constrained development of the Indian–U.S. relationship. The dialogue between Jaswant Singh, India's external affairs minister, and Strobe Talbott, former U.S. deputy secretary of state, has demonstrated, however, that the two governments can conduct business more productively. The United States should cooperate with India to reduce nuclear dangers in two ways. First, India and the United States should reassure each other about their nuclear policies. India should amplify its conception of a minimal nuclear deterrent and delineate more clearly its system of command and control. The United States should lift the sanctions—triggered by India's nuclear testing—which are accomplishing little. Further, the two sides should find a way to resume civilian nuclear cooperation. If the United States can sign a nuclear accord with North Korea, it can cooperate with India to improve the safety of its nuclear plants. An urgent priority is the need to shut down the unsafe U.S.-built Tarapur plant and improve the safety of other facilities.

Second, opportunities for collaboration abound in global disarmament and arms control. India supports the idea of nuclear weapons abolition; similarly, the Bush administration may make deep cuts in strategic nuclear forces. Indian officials and some U.S. analysts have advocated de-alerting nuclear forces.[2] The United States seems determined to deploy missile defenses, which may affect India, particularly if China reacts adversely. The United States and India could jointly promote a nuclear regime that combines reducing U.S. and Russian strategic nuclear forces, de-alerting nuclear weapons worldwide, and sharing missile defense technologies.

Beyond nuclear issues, Washington has an opportunity to contribute to India's continuing defense modernization, which cyclically peaks every 20 years. After major arms purchases in the late 1970s, New Delhi is again shopping for military hardware, this time from diverse suppliers. Unfortunately, the post-Pokhran sanctions impede U.S. arms sales to India. The sanctions, having outlived their effectiveness, should be scrapped. After sanctions are lifted, the United States should initiate a mature arms relationship with New Delhi to strengthen Indian security, to eliminate lingering fears of U.S. animosity, and to enlist India in managing global security.

In an everyday sense, India's security is threatened far more by Pakistan than by China. Although India rejects formal third-party mediation, it wants the United States to use its influence with Islamabad to resolve the Kashmir conflict. Washington should insist that Pakistan restrain the separatists so that India can negotiate seriously with Islamabad and Kashmiri leaders. Engagement at the economic, developmental, and political levels in Pakistan, however, must accompany U.S. pressure on Islamabad. The United States can contribute to defusing the problems in Pakistan by playing an economic benefactor role, given the parlous state of Pakistan's economy; a developmental role in fortifying Pakistan's educational system against the *madrassahs*; and a political role in curbing the extremist officers in the military.

The United States should continue talks with India on Asian security—particularly China—by working with New Delhi to construct an OSCE-type security structure for Asia. An Organization for Security and Cooperation in Asia (OSCA) should recognize basic realities: that China is situated at the heart of Asia, with lengthy borders and interests in all the regions abutting it, and that Beijing feels threatened by its neighbors as much as it is a threat to them. An OSCA would reassure both China and its neighbors and would also help regulate the interactions among the biggest powers in Asia—China, India, Japan, Russia, and the United States—that are increasingly intertwined across the continent. The ASEAN Regional Forum (ARF) is the kernel of an OSCA, but the ARF's membership is restricted to the eastern theater of Asia and the Asia–Pacific region. India is a member of the ARF; the rest of South Asia is not. Central Asia has shown some interest in a security forum and is also outside the ARF sphere of activity. South Asia, Central Asia, and the Asia–Pacific region should be brought together to manage security interdependencies that increasingly stretch across the face of the continent.

Finally, the United States should support India's candidacy for a permanent seat on the UN Security Council. UN reform and expansion of the Security Council is a vexing issue. Washington has indicated it would support Security Council membership for Germany and Japan, but Indians feel strongly that any future expansion should accommodate their country. India possesses various qualifications for a seat. Millions of Indian troops fought on the winning side of both world wars. In addition, thousands of Indian troops have served the international community since 1947 as peacekeepers. Their experience, their skill at law and order as well as battlefield operations, and their discipline make them ideal "blue helmets." India was present at the UN's creation and has participated fully in the workings of the world organization. Indians have served with distinction throughout the UN bureaucracy. India has also, without fail, paid its annual dues. New Delhi is willing to increase its responsibility, especially as a permanent member of the Security Council, but also if not invited to become one. Democratic India is an invaluable UN member, and its democratic system is the envy of, and model for, the developing world. As a full-franchise mass democracy since 1947, the vitality of India's noisy political system, despite horrendously difficult conditions, deserves recognition. Finally, the absence of a country representing one-fifth of humanity at the high table of international relations is an anomaly that should be rectified.

Economics

The United States at present has relatively small trade and investment interests in India. Yet, the economic relationship has grown steadily over the past decade. India's one billion consumers are a lure, even though their purchasing power remains limited. Sustained by 7 percent annual growth rates and doubling per capita incomes every 10 years, the Indian market could be highly lucrative.[3]

The most radical step toward a closer economic relationship between the United States and India is a free-trade area (FTA). Although India is a member of the World Trade Organization (WTO) and is committed to nondiscriminatory trade relations, and although a bilateral FTA may not be unequivocally good, proceeding with such an arrangement could benefit both countries. For India, an FTA could help counter economic discrimination it faces in trade flows because of its exclusion from most preferential trade groups. In the wake of the 1999 WTO conference in Seattle, an FTA could also serve India well until the multilateral negotiating track resumes in earnest.[4] It could boost textile and clothing exports, increase the mobility of skilled Indian technical personnel, raise levels of foreign direct investment, reinvigorate domestic economic reforms, and spark the interest of other trading partners, such as the EU, in India. For the United States, an FTA would give U.S. firms early entry into a large market. The FTA would also provide a framework for resolving trade issues relating to intellectual property rights, pharmaceuticals, and labor and environmental standards.[5]

Until the U.S.–Indian relationship matures to this point, the new administration should promote India's entry into the Asia–Pacific Economic Cooperation (APEC) forum. Indian economic reforms have largely removed the economic hurdles to membership. In the long run, India's growth and financial stability will contribute to the prosperity and vitality of the region. The last APEC expansion excluded India, but a number of countries in Asia have been sympathetic to its near-term candidacy. New Delhi wants to move out of its restricted South Asian role and has already crafted a more creative diplomacy toward the Asia–Pacific region. India's membership in APEC would ultimately give it a greater say in this superregion and would serve U.S. interests: India clearly has more stamina and balancing power against the giants of the region than the smaller states of East and Southeast Asia.

Finally, the United States should make India—as well as Brazil and China—dialogue partners of the Group of Seven. All three countries will surpass the smaller G-7 members in absolute economic size, making their full membership in the elite club imperative. Bringing them into the club may take time, so the process should begin now. Globalization with a human face, as Clinton suggested after the street protests in Seattle, is the challenge of the future. Brazil, China, and India can contribute to a fruitful conversation over globalization, and the time to begin that conversation has arrived.

Energy

The new U.S. administration should address the issue of energy cooperation with India in the crucial areas of coal, hydroelectricity, oil, and natural gas.[6] U.S. involvement could transform not just India's energy prospects but also those of the entire region. The last time the United States became involved in South Asia's energy problems, India and Pakistan reached agreement on the disposition of the shared Indus rivers. Forty years later, the United States should once again play a major developmental role in the region.

Coal is India's primary fuel, contributing 64 percent of India's power generation. Unfortunately, India's coal is poor quality, with a high ash content. The United States could help India use its coal more efficiently and make it ecologically more sustainable. Clean coal technologies, specifically designed for high ash content, are the answer. Indian engineering companies, research institutions, and public utilities, as well as various U.S. public and private entities, could combine to develop the appropriate systems. The Indian Ministry of Power and the U.S. Department of Energy could act as facilitators. Indian funding of its public utilities and U.S. Export–Import Bank loans for U.S. companies would be crucial. Similarly, India and the United States could collaborate to improve Indian coal mining practices and equipment.[7]

India has enormous undeveloped hydroelectric capacity; at a load factor of 60 percent, India may have as much as 84,044 megawatts of hydroelectric potential, of which only 27 percent has been realized.[8] Hydroelectric power—properly developed, with due attention to the rehabilitation of displaced persons and to environmental dangers—is India's greatest energy source, one that will long outlast global oil supplies. It represents the single most important investment in India's development and security. The United States could play a major role in mobilizing multilateral funding for, and the engineering and construction of, a series of projects.[9]

The United States can play a low-key but crucial role in India's oil problem, too. India depends on imports for 70 percent of its oil. New Delhi's perennial concerns are reliability of supplies and price stability, both of which would be alleviated by a pipeline connecting India to the Persian Gulf via Pakistan. The most important U.S. contribution would be allowing Iranian participation in the pipeline's construction and operation. Without U.S. acquiescence to Iran joining a consortium, international financing of such a massive scheme would be politically doomed. An ancillary benefit of the scheme, which coincides with the United States' long-term interest, would be to give India, Iran, and Pakistan a stake in each other's security and well-being.

Much more significant, however, is the U.S. interest in exploiting the natural gas resources of South Asia. By all accounts, the recently discovered Bangladeshi deposits are commercially most viable if a market larger than the Bangladeshi domestic market can be found. India is that market: it is energy deficient—its own reserves will be depleted in 30 years—and eager to buy from a reliable source. Bangladesh's massive reserves (variously estimated at 20–60 trillion cubic feet) and location make it the ideal energy partner. U.S. companies are already active in Bangladesh: their investments in the natural gas sector could amount to $3 billion in the coming years. Bilateral differences between India and Bangladesh have clouded the relationship and account for Bangladeshi reluctance to sell to India, but Washington could play a constructive role in bringing Dhaka to the negotiating table.[10] Given the magnitude of the reserves, India is not the only market for Bangladeshi gas; Sri Lanka, Thailand, and others in Southeast Asia are potential buyers as well. U.S. cooperation with India could center on a "Bay of Bengal Community" with a focus on energy and trade.

Ecology

India and the United States should cooperate on global warming and India's own environmental problems. In January 2001, for the first time, an international consortium of scientists agreed that human actions were responsible for the increase in global warming and that the consequences of not rectifying the situation could be calamitous.[11] At the same time, India's environment continues to decay and risk the lives of more than one billion people and the stability of neighboring countries and regions.

The United States is still the largest contributing factor to global warming, although India is also contributing to the problem. In 1995,

India ranked sixth in the world in carbon dioxide emissions and produced 3.6 percent of the global total.[12] The United States must reduce its carbon emissions much faster than it has done so far, but other countries such as Brazil, China, and India must step up their control efforts as well. A global compact is vital. The developed countries must find a way to transfer to other countries the technologies that will reduce carbon emissions worldwide. In return, the developing countries must limit their emissions more strictly.

The United States leads the rich states, and India has championed the cause of the poorer nations, when environmental concerns are discussed. Washington and New Delhi should work with, rather than against, each other. First, they should explore how to implement the Kyoto Protocol as speedily as possible. Scientists are converging on two key remedial measures: forest and other land conservation efforts and the trading of "emission credits." India and the United States should focus on fashioning a concrete program of international action based on these ideas and others.[13] Second, India and the rest of the G-15, as well as China, should develop an interim agreement with the G-8 countries. This action plan would solve the bulk of the emissions problem. Washington should immediately confer with New Delhi (and others) on reinvigorating the multilateral Kyoto process and convening a joint meeting of the G-15 and G-8.

India is home to virtually every ecological problem imaginable, but the most severe difficulty is water scarcity.[14] One U.S. estimate has India "fast reaching the crisis stage. Population and economic growth will diminish per capita water availability by 75 percent by 2025."[15] More than 200 million people inhabit water deficient areas; an additional 222 million live in areas with a teetering balance between water supply and demand.[16] Possible recession of the Himalayan glaciers, the increase in freshwater pollution (already 70 percent polluted), the doubling of water demand by 2005 (in comparison to the early 1990s), and the changing claims on water supplies (between agriculture, industry, and households) are some of the factors that could produce an acute scarcity of water.[17] The consequences of water shortages could be considerable. Water scarcity plus "adverse environmental conditions, worsening air pollution, ... and continued land degradation" could mean a shortfall in cereal production of 36–140 million tons by 2010.[18]

Allowing for uncertainty and some alarmism, the picture presented is still frightening. To satisfy future demand, India needs to increase the supply of water and to improve water conservation. The United States can be helpful in both tasks. Improved mapping of India's water resources is one major area of cooperation. Better boring and pump technologies could help tap more groundwater. Irrigation systems could be more efficient so that the agricultural sector, the largest user of water, can reduce waste. U.S. experience in wastewater pollution control could be applied to increase the availability of potable water. The U.S. Agency for International Development (USAID) could help develop a pricing mechanism for rural water use. Charging consumers for water would encourage a more rational allocation of hydrological resources and would generate revenues for water conservation projects.

Epidemics

India is a key country in the control of infectious diseases worldwide. With its huge population, it is a central battleground in the fight against various epidemics. In particular, India may be the next great AIDS tragedy, following Africa. The United States has an interest—strategically, economically, and medically—in confronting and combating the spread of AIDS. A partnership with India will serve the interests of both countries.

India has 3.7 million people who are HIV-positive; in the early 1990s, that figure was just a few thousand. The HIV "prevalence rate" in India is 0.7 percent, that is, 7 in 1,000 people in the 15–49 age group are infected.[19] Overall, this rate of infection is relatively low. In some Indian states, however, the rate is already 1–2 percent.[20] A crucial age cohort is the 12–20 age group that will soon enter a sexually active phase. Millions in this cohort could pass the virus to sexual partners and children. HIV prevalence could increase dramatically as a result.

The Indian HIV/AIDS epidemic is closer to the sub-Saharan African model than the Western pattern. HIV is transmitted primarily through heterosexual contact, including the use of commercial sex workers, and through injected drug use. The mother-to-child transmission rate is also significant; prenatal surveillance shows that the infection rate among pregnant women is 3.3–6.5 percent.[21] In addition, India's blood supply is not adequately protected and is contributing to the spread of HIV. A number of factors could increase the susceptibility and vulnerability of the Indian population to HIV. Poverty, illiteracy, lack of basic health care, growing infection in women, income disparities, growing physical mobility, and the continuing social stigma of HIV could accelerate the gallop of the disease.

The United States clearly has an interest in helping to control the spread of HIV in India for moral and humanitarian reasons, but there are more material motivations as well. For more than 50 years, India has been a bulwark of political stability in Asia. A full-blown HIV epidemic could devastate India, undermine its political fabric, and jeopardize peace throughout the region. Economically, an HIV epidemic on an African scale would be devastating. Disability and death from HIV/AIDS could severely retard development.[22] Finally, the more HIV spreads, the harder it will become to predict the precise forms it takes. Mutations of the virus could be more lethal than present strains. The fight against HIV/AIDS could become even more costly and complex as a result.

What should the United States do in India's HIV struggle? First, it should help fund better surveillance of HIV. India has only 180 "sentinel surveillance sites" and plans to conduct surveillance only once a year, [23] which is inadequate for a country of one billion people. U.S. funding for improved surveillance could be channeled through USAID and the Joint UN Program on HIV/AIDS (UNAIDS). Second, Washington should encourage the Indian government to make the HIV epidemic a higher priority in its health and social policies, specifically urging India to form a high-level task force to oversee the fight against HIV. This task force should bring together representatives of a wide array of government agencies including those responsible for health, education, finance, planning, women's welfare, and defense. It should also have representatives of nongovernmental organizations that work on HIV-related issues. Third, the U.S. government should encourage U.S. businesses that operate in India to become involved in the fight against HIV. U.S. companies could distribute free condoms to their workers as well as information pamphlets to workers' families and offer voluntary testing, with a nondisclosure policy, and spousal support. Fourth, the United States should promote collaboration between its scientific community and health professionals and their Indian counterparts. The two countries' national task forces on HIV/AIDS could organize this joint effort. One vital area of cooperation is improving India's blood banks.

Last but not least, the U.S. and Indian governments should work together to make life-saving drugs financially affordable for HIV-infected patients. Comprehensive pricing regimes, covering the treatment of opportunistic infections and the use of antiretroviral drugs (where adequate monitoring is available), could be negotiated to make medical costs more affordable.[24] Fortunately, the major drug companies are already examining price reductions for drugs for the most desperate countries. In addition, India and the United States could reach an agreement whereby Indian companies, such as Cipla, could manufacture "generic" antiretrovirals at much lower cost for the Indian market and for the worst-hit countries in Asia and Africa, with the pharmaceutical multinationals compensated at a reasonable rate.

Partnership for the Future

In the decades to come, the security and welfare of India, with its one-billion-plus people, will have great consequences for the international system. Under these circumstances, the action program outlined here becomes inescapable. The United States has a direct economic interest and a more indirect political interest in cooperating with this Big Emerging Market. An India that turns the corner by improving its security and welfare will be an enormous force for good in international society.

That potential is both the premise and the promise of an Indian–U.S. strategic partnership in the decades to come.

Notes

1. *India–U.S. Relations: A Vision for the 21st Century*, Embassy of India, Washington, D.C., located at <http://www.indianembassy.org/indusrel/clinton_india/home.html> (Joint India–U.S. statement).

2. Harold A. Feiveson, ed., *The Nuclear Turning Point: A Blueprint for Deep Cuts and De-Alerting of Nuclear Weapons* (Washington, D.C.: Brookings Institution Press, 1999).

3. Ten percent of India's imports go to the United States; 20 percent of its imports are from the United States. Also, 20 percent of its foreign direct investment comes from the United States. Indian exports and imports are only 1 percent of U.S. totals. See Aaditya Mattoo and Arvind Subramanian, "A Free Trade Area of the Democracies?" in Kanti P. Bajpai and Amitabh Mattoo, eds., *Engaged Democracies: India–US Relations in the 21st Century* (New Delhi: Har Anand, 2000), 53–54.

4. Mattoo and Subramanian, "A Free Trade Area of the Democracies?" 53–62.

5. Ibid., 60–61 (labor and environmental standards in a U.S.–India FTA).

6. The United States could sell nuclear power reactors to India. Given the economic, environmental, and social costs of nuclear energy, however, this option is not attractive.

7. A. Gopalakrishnan, "The Potential for Indo–U.S. Cooperation in the Electric Power Sector," in Bajpai and Mattoo, eds., *Engaged Democracies*, 85–104. Dr. Gopalakrishnan was chairman of India 's Atomic Energy Regulatory Board (AERB) from 1993–1996.

8. Ibid., 94.

9. Ibid., 93–95.

10. Ibid., 95–97.

11. Andrew C. Revkin, "Report to Endorse Expanding Forests to Fight Warming," *New York Times*, February 10, 2001.

12. DCI Environmental Center, "India's Environmental Challenges," *Environmental Report Series* (Washington, D.C., March 2000), 8.

13. Revkin, "Report to Endorse Expanding Forests to Fight Warming."

14. See DCI, "India's Environmental Challenges."

15. Ibid., iii.

16. Calculations based on figure 3 in DCI, "India's Environmental Challenges."

17. DCI, "India's Environmental Challenges," 1, 4–7.

18. Ibid., iii, 11.

19. UNAIDS, *Report on the Global HIV/AIDS Epidemic* (June 2000), 128.

20. In South Africa, infection rates rose from less than 1 percent in the early 1990s to 20 percent in less than a decade. See Monitoring the AIDS Pandemic (MAP), *The Status and Trends of the HIV/AIDS Epidemics in the World*, July 5–7, 2000, 3, located at <http://www.census.gov/ipc/www/hivdurbn.html> (provisional report).

21. UNAIDS, *Report on the Global HIV/AIDS Epidemic*, 130.

22. *Review of the Problem of Human Immunodeficiency Virus/Acquired Immunodeficiency Syndrome in All Its Aspects*, Special Session of the General Assembly on HIV/AIDS, Report to the Secretary General, A/55/779 (February 16, 2001), 8. The report notes, "If the epidemic continues at its present rate, the hardest-hit nations stand to lose up to 25 percent of their projected economic growth over the next 20 years." Ibid., 4, located at <http://www.unaids.org/whatsnew/others/un_special/SGreport1.doc>.

23. Monitoring the AIDS Pandemic (MAP), *The Status and Trends of HIV/AIDS/STD in Asia and the Pacific*, October 23, 1999, 10 (provisional report), located at <http://www.census.gov/ipc/www/hivkuala.html>.

24. On Brazil's resort to antiretrovirals, see Tina Rosenberg, "Look at Brazil," *New York Times Magazine*, January 28, 2001, 26–31, 52, 58, 62–63. Brazil may have saved many lives and up to $1 billion from 1997–1999 through antiretroviral therapy. Durban MAP, *The Status and Trends of the HIV/AIDS Epidemics in the World*, 8.

Chong Guan Kwa and See Seng Tan

The Keystone of World Order

In September 1901, President William McKinley addressed the new century's world trade fair in Buffalo, New York, declaring, "God and men have linked nations together [and] no nation can longer be indifferent to any other." McKinley's attempt to move his country away from George Washington's advice, to avoid entering any "entangling alliance," was unfortunately preempted by his assassination the following day. That task fell to his successor, Theodore Roosevelt, to get the United States to recognize "the increasing interdependence and complexity of international political and economic relations [that] render it incumbent on all civilised and orderly powers to insist on the proper policing of the world." Forcing the United States to assist with the "proper policing of the world" took the next half-century. During that time, everyone had to endure U.S. efforts to police and protect the world against the dangers of communism.

Should the United States, at the dawn of a new century, heed George Washington's call to withdraw from all entangling alliances or, alternatively, others' advice to consolidate its Cold War victory, become the primary global power, and prevent the rise of any rival? What kind of

Chong Guan Kwa and See Seng Tan are, respectively, head of external programs and assistant professor at the Institute of Defense and Strategic Studies in Singapore.

Copyright © 2001 by The Center for Strategic and International Studies and the Massachusetts Institute of Technology
The Washington Quarterly • 24:3 pp. 95–103.

role would we, the countries of Southeast Asia, wish to see the United States play, that of a withdrawn and isolated follower or an assertive and hegemonic global power? A highly desirable role for the United States in East Asia would be as the "keystone" of the world order, and more specifically of the East Asian region.[1] For the most part, Europeans treat the notion of sustained U.S. engagement in world affairs with either ambivalence or outright disdain. The mood in East Asia—with the possible exception of China—is significantly different.

Traditional U.S. allies—Japan, South Korea, Taiwan, Australia, New Zealand, and Singapore—have long perceived the United States as the region's great stabilizer and "honest broker," albeit not a disinterested one. The end of the Cold War did little to change this perception, notwithstanding the forced closure of U.S. bases in the Philippines. At the time, rampant fears of an imminent reduction in the U.S. military presence compelled a senior State Department official in 1991 to allay Asian concerns of Washington's intentions. "Our adaptation to new circumstances must not be interpreted as withdrawal. America's destiny lies across the Pacific; our engagement in the region is here to stay."[2] East Asians, for the most part, acknowledge the value of the United States as a "virtual buffer state" among the interests, actual or perceived, of regional powers such as China, Japan, and the two Koreas. The possibility that this perceived value might dissipate in the foreseeable future is highly unlikely, particularly in light of an ascending China.

Nonetheless, casting the United States as the region's keystone or pillar is not without problems. After all, the United States is, among many other things, the land of the Monroe Doctrine and Madonna, where modern faith in the possibility of radical disjuncture from Old World cynicism (the doctrine) shares space with the postmodern virtue of endless reinventions of identity (the artiste). U.S. "exceptionalism" may be grasped as emancipation from the fetters of history; in a sense, it is to rewrite history by reinventing the United States and, by extension, the world. We recall, for example, Madeleine Albright's impassioned plea, issued at her Senate confirmation hearings, that "we [the

United States] must be more than audience, more even than actors; we must be the authors of the history of our age."[3]

On one hand, such high-minded ambition—some would even say arrogance—is anathema to many East Asians,[4] especially those who take issue with the evangelistic zeal of U.S. foreign policy makers to remake East Asia into an annex of Americana, or, failing that, an authoritarian Other: modern in the economic sense, but primitive in social and political realms. On the other hand, the fundamental significance of the U.S. presence in East Asia is unquestionable—a fact that East Asian politicians and pundits grudgingly acknowledge. Surely, criticisms of hypocrisy leveled against East Asian regimes are not entirely without justification.[5] For example, throughout the "Asian values debate," these regimes were criticized for rejecting U.S. demands for liberal democracy and human rights protection in their countries, but accepting, or even insisting on, U.S. military protection and support for their territories. Notably, Singaporean contributions to that debate for the most part did not advocate the superiority of Asian values as much as "react to Western proselytiz[ing]."[6] Exporting democracy and other liberal values is beneficial when tempered by an appreciation for the difficulties involved in transplanting political practices into a variety of historical and geographical contexts.[7]

The United States apparently understands this role, at least in foreign policy rhetoric if not in actual foreign policy practice. Warning "the enemies of liberty and our country" against presuming any imminent isolationist turn in U.S. foreign policy, President George W. Bush intimated in his inauguration speech that "America remains engaged in the world, *by history and by choice*, shaping a balance of power that favors freedom."[8] By these words, the president clearly means U.S. freedom. A United States as keystone of the "East Asian order," however, precisely because of its deep appreciation for the interrelation of history and choice, may be required on occasion to regulate or restrain its own freedom voluntarily in the interests of international stability, similar to what Indonesia under Suharto had done for regional stability in Southeast Asia during the formative period of the Association of Southeast Asian Nations (ASEAN).[9]

Sharing the president's evident sensitivity for the U.S. role in the region—though not necessarily his policy preferences or his policy execution—we imagine the United States as a key regional pillar that exercises power and prerogative in accordance with its own interests, but with a fundamental appreciation for moderation and restraint and a deep sensitivity to the region's immense complexities. The stakes are enormous; as a scholar once warned, East Asia, more than any other region in the post–Cold War era, constitutes a potential "cockpit of great-power conflict."[10] Clearly, whatever the ideal regional role for the United States is, it does not consist of pushing East Asia toward that calamitous end.

The Unbearable "Lightness" of U.S. Leadership

François Heisbourg has usefully identified four visions of the United States that more or less comport with the ways in which non-U.S.— certainly European—public opinion views the United States in its conduct of foreign policy: "benign hegemon;" "rogue state;" "trigger-happy sheriff;" and "keystone of world order."[11] Given the usually generous image of the United States held by many East Asians, the more odious of Heisbourg's visions may not apply, at least not historically. If the ambivalence in regional news editorials is indicative, however, an incipient sense of unease among East Asians lingers over recent U.S. conduct in East Asia, rendering those visions plausible.

French foreign minister Hubert Védrine's description of the United States as a hyperpower (*hyperpuissance*) implies that a benign hegemon (or, in another formulation, "benevolent empire") can at times appear to others as an insufferable bully.[12] Much of this perception involves Washington's post–Cold War gravitation toward a unilateralist foreign policy, notwithstanding President Bill Clinton's stated preference for "assertive multilateralism." Prior to the North Atlantic Treaty Organization (NATO) air campaign against Yugoslavia in the spring of 1999, for example, several European leaders objected to alleged U.S. hubris and its tendency "to go it alone." As Stewart Patrick has observed, since the end of the Cold War, the United States "has demonstrated a growing willingness to act alone and to opt out of multilateral initiatives."[13] A capricious regard for multilateralism, Patrick concluded, may complicate U.S. formulation and pursuit of a coherent foreign policy.[14] Most recently, Washington's unilateral impulse manifested itself in the Bush team's insistence in the face of fierce opposition from strategic allies and others to proceed with plans to build and, conceivably in the near future, operate national missile defense (NMD) and theatre missile defense (TMD) systems.

Second, the notion of a rogue state, thanks to recent trends in U.S. foreign policy, naturally conjures an image of Iraq, Iran, or North Korea. As farfetched as the idea of the United States as a rogue state may seem, certain East Asian quarters are growing more concerned about U.S. "revisionist" tendencies, in the sense that the United States seeks to undermine the regional status quo. As U.S. national security adviser Condoleezza Rice opined, "Great powers do not just mind their own business."[15] A key to this observation is the recent U.S. redefinition of China as a "strategic competitor" rather than, as had been the case for Bush's predecessor, a "strategic partner." In comparison with Clinton's engagement model, the differences in Bush's policy, as Secretary of State Colin Powell has taken pains to note, are more apparent than real, especially vis-à-vis trade issues. More disturbing, however, is unabashed U.S. support for Taiwan, an especially vexatious issue for China.

Equally troubling is the movement toward using Japan as an ally for balancing China. The so-called U.S.–Japan–China "trialogue" has an element of déjà vu,[16] bringing back memories (unwanted for some, perhaps) of Henry Kissinger's triangular, great-power balance, which involved the United States teaming with China against the Soviet Union.[17] Although this activity surely is insufficient evidence to merit categorizing the United States as a malign hegemon, the unfortunate image of a dominant power willfully employing its vast assets and power to achieve its own ends—without much concern for what John Ikenberry has termed "strategic restraint"—implies a certain roguishness to its behavior. From this vantage point, Rice's position that "China is not a 'status quo' power" because it "resents the role of the United States in the Asia–Pacific region" clearly has an odd ring to it, because a similar charge can be made of the "revisionist" U.S. stance.[18]

The third vision brings a cheeky twist to Richard Haass's notion of the United States as a "reluctant sheriff" uneasy with the clarion call to guarantee world order in the post–Cold War era.[19] A host of post–Cold War militaristic adventures—Panama; the Persian Gulf; Serbia; Kosovo; and most recently under Bush, the bombing of Iraqi targets—has encouraged the perception abroad of a trigger-happy sheriff. According to this view, the notion of U.S. reluctance to police the world is contested less on strategic grounds than on the U.S. proclivity toward a highly selective, incoherent policy. Hence, this sheriff is both quick on the trigger and fickle and unreliable, as U.S. indecisiveness over Bosnia in the early 1990s implied. Washington's unwillingness to risk U.S. lives in the pursuit of less than vital interests—an otherwise legitimate concern—may force the impression that, in games of "chicken," the United States would invariably blink first. Such perceptions of U.S. unreliability, whether or not correct, could prove disastrous for its East Asian allies, some of whom, such as South Korea and Taiwan, face highly unstable and unpredictable situations.

The fourth and final vision of the United States as the keystone or pillar of world order is not mutually exclusive of the earlier three visions. Many Europeans—and, needless to say, East Asians—still regard the U.S. role as salient to the existing international order. In other words, the United States is perceived as "the only credible ultimate guarantor of that order" and the "only global-scale exporter of security."[20] Complaints of U.S. roguishness or trigger-happy behavior aside, there remains the strong if painful awareness that, if not for the existing security framework provided by bilateral and multilateral alliance commitments borne by the United States, the world could, or perhaps would, be a more perilous place.

Speaking of the relative success of alliances and other institutional frameworks, however, presupposes the existence of norms, principles, and rules. John Gerard Ruggie, for example, has argued that there exists, among the developed nations since the end of the Great Depression of the 1930s, a "common social purpose" to eschew the market failure of the depression period by ensuring the maintenance of a liberal economic order.[21] Ruggie called that common social purpose "embedded liberalism." No nation, benign hegemons included, can successfully manage international order without the consensual support of other nations that results from a shared social purpose—unless, of course, it rules by fiat. How a common social purpose can emerge and be embedded without multilateral engagement by the parties involved is admittedly difficult to imagine. Whether Washington can sufficiently restrain itself from an excessive unilateral impulse and engender the necessary social and political capital for the role of guarantor of international order is unclear, as is whether Washington, under Bush, views pursuing such a role as desirable in the first place.

In contrast to Europe, East Asia has no corresponding alliance commitments and institutions. In this respect, the most ambitious and extensive framework in the region today, the ASEAN Regional Forum (ARF), is precisely that—a security forum, or "talk shop," not a defense arrangement. Worse yet is the uncertainty about how the Bush administration's reticence over multilateralism in East Asia would affect the future of the ARF. The recent flap over the commander in chief of the U.S. Pacific Command Admiral Dennis Blair's idea of forming "security communities" in East Asia rendered explicit to the Bush administration the ostensible wisdom of its stated reliance on (in Powell's words) "the bedrock" of bilateral alliances to cement U.S. influence in the region.

"Alliances," as Bush's campaign-trail mantra went, "are not just for crises." This stance also places doubt on the future of Blair's "parallel diplomacy," which, by most accounts, has achieved some genuine progress in the promotion of multilateral cooperative security in East Asia. In fairness, not only Washington's reluctance regarding multilateral engagement is at issue here. Some East Asians are tepid toward prospects of further multilateralization in their own backyard, as evidenced by Chinese suspicions over the alleged U.S. effort to "contain

China," or the overworked rationalizations of some ASEAN member nations regarding the importance of doing business "the ASEAN way." Nor, as some have argued, do East Asian countries have the kind of common social purpose that is found among their European counterparts.[22] Nonetheless, what most of East Asia does seem to have, as noted earlier, is an appreciation for the United States as the region's stabilizer and honest broker for mediating regional relations in an interested but, for the most part, fair way.

U.S. Self-Images and Adopted Roles

Whatever hopes we in Southeast Asia may have for the United States will ultimately have to correspond to U.S. images of its role. Without links between our hopes and U.S. aspirations, our hopes become illusory. On a personal level, no one who switches on a personal computer today to log on to the Internet is unaware of the power of U.S. technology. Everyone who invests in stocks watches with interest and concern the cycles of the Nasdaq index. At the national level, we scrutinize the pronouncements of Alan Greenspan for its possible impact on our economies. This economic preponderance and technological singularity gives the United States the wherewithal to manage its relations with the rest of the world unilaterally. On the other hand, doubts about its ability to police the world and its preoccupation with domestic issues—particularly drugs, crime, and the environment—might lead the United States to look inward rather than outward. As in the 1930s, the option to isolate itself from the problems of the world may appear increasingly attractive.[23]

Most of Southeast Asia would not want to see the United States go home. Indeed, one of the implicit goals of the ARF is keeping the United States engaged in the Asia–Pacific region. The challenge of this task is ensuring that the United States is a self-restrained power and does not become a "rogue" superpower that the rest of the world must then contain.

Robert Zoellick, Bush's erudite trade representative, has cogently argued that a key presidential responsibility is to produce "a strategy that will shape the world so as to protect and promote U.S. interests for the next 50 years."[24] Notwithstanding the otherwise legitimate concerns of East Asian powers that resist intrusion, the United States does have legitimate interests in East Asia that need to be protected and promoted. The traditional view from Singapore—a "small red dot on the map," as a former regional leader reminded us—is well represented by Lee Kuan Yew, who asserted in 1966 that, "in the last resort, it is power which decides what happens and, therefore, it behooves us to ensure that we always have overwhelming power on our side." As the guarantor of world order, the United States partly underwrites the survival of small states such as Singapore. More importantly, we believe that Washington, in promoting its vision of the U.S. role in the twenty-first century, must necessarily exercise a generous measure of restraint. Washington has completed this task so well in the postwar period, even as it pursued the Herculean task of stabilizing the world order. For the most part, current U.S. East Asian policy seems to lack precisely this element of self-moderation. Inis Claude, a prominent scholar of the balance of power system, in summing up his decades-long study of the balance of power principle vis-à-vis the European order, wrote:

> That this moderation is viewed as the essential foundation for the functioning of the balance of power system rather than as a consequence of its functioning is evidenced by the fact that the fading and ultimate collapse of the efficacy of that system is customarily attributed to the decline of those factors that sustained moderation.[25]

The world of present-day East Asia is quite different from nineteenth-century Europe, but the wisdom of Claude's reflections on moderation and power balancing still hold true. Bush has spoken passionately on U.S. engagement in the world as primarily about "shaping a balance of power that favours freedom."[27] We argue that the United States and its East Asian counterparts can properly realize the collective aim of freedom in the judicious pursuit of U.S. interests in East Asia within the role of guarantor and stabilizer of the regional order. The alternative—the United States as an unrestrained, untutored, roguish bully, particularly in a region as fragile, unpredictable, and yet so full of promise as contemporary East Asia—would simply and surely be disastrous not only for East Asia, but also for the United States.

Notes

1. See François Heisbourg, "American Hegemony? Perceptions of the U.S. Abroad," *Survival* 41, no. 4 (Winter 1999–2000): 5–19.

2. Richard Solomon, former U.S. assistant secretary of state for East Asia and the Pacific, made this point during a visit to Auckland, New Zealand, in 1991. *Straits Times*, August 7, 1991.

3. Martin Walker, "Present at the Solution: Madeleine Albright's Ambitious Foreign Policy," *World Policy Institute* 14, no. 1 (1997): 2.

4. William Overholt, for instance, is scathing in his condemnation of Albright's tenure as the top U.S. diplomat, particularly her knowledge and policy toward East Asia. See William H. Overholt, "Bush and Asia: Solid, Centrist," *Nomura: Asia Strategy* (December 28, 2000), 2.

5. See, for example, Eric Jones, "Asia's Fate," *National Interest* 35 (Spring 1994): 18–28.

6. Kishore Mahbubani, "Preface," in *Can Asians Think?* (Singapore: Times Books International, 1998), 11.

7. We are reminded here of the moral realism of Reinhold Niebuhr, who once cautioned his fellow Americans, "We [the United States] cannot simply have our way, not even when we believe our way to have the 'happiness of mankind' as its promise." Ibid., 12.

8. Lee Siew Hua, "Bush Pledges to Keep the U.S. Engaged with the World," *Straits Times*, January 22, 2001, 1 (emphasis added).

9. See, for example, Arnfinn Jorgensen-Dahl, *Regional Organization and Order in Southeast Asia* (London: Macmillan, 1982).

10. Richard K. Betts, "Wealth, Power, and Instability: East Asia and the United States after the Cold War," *International Security* 18 (1993/1994): 64.

11. Heisbourg, "American Hegemony?".

12. Robert Kagan, "The Benevolent Empire," *Foreign Policy* (Summer 1998); Heisbourg, "American Hegemony?" 9.

13. Stewart Patrick, "America's Retreat from Multilateral Engagement," *Current History* 99 (December 2000): 430–439.

14. Ibid., p. 437.

15. Condoleezza Rice, "Promoting the National Interest," *Foreign Affairs* 79, no. 1 (January/February 2000): 49.

16. U.S. Institute of Peace, *"Trialogue": U.S.–Japan–China Relations and Asian–Pacific Stability* (Washington, D.C.: U.S. Institute of Peace, 1998).

17. See, for example, Richard K. Ashley, *The Political Economy of War and Peace: The Sino–Soviet–American Triangle and the Modern Security Problematique* (London: Frances Pinter, 1980).

18. Rice, "Promoting the National Interest," 56.

19. Richard N. Haass, *The Reluctant Sheriff: The United States after the Cold War* (New York: Brookings Institution, 1998).

20. Heisbourg, "American Hegemony?" 15–16.

21. John Gerard Ruggie, "International Regimes, Transactions, and Change: Embedded Liberalism in the Postwar Economic Order," in Stephen D. Krasner, ed., *International Regimes* (Ithaca, N.Y.: Cornell University Press, 1983), 198.

22. As Sheldon Simon has written concerning, in his view, the Asia–Pacific region (and, by implication, East Asia as well):

    No real *community* consisting of common values, interlocking histories, and the free movement of peoples and firms across national boundaries exists yet in the region. Hence the reticence about creating political institutions that would entail policymaking based on legal procedures. Successful institutions require common views of objectives as well as cost and benefit sharing.

    Sheldon W. Simon, "Security, Economic Liberalism, and Democracy: Asian Elite Perceptions of Post–Cold War Foreign Policy Values," *NBR Analysis* 7, no. 2 (Summer 1996): 5–32.

23. See, for example, the essays debating "restraint," "selective engagement," "cooperative security," and "primacy" as alternative frameworks for analyzing U.S. strategic choices in M. E. Brown et al, *America's Strategic Choices, An International Security Reader* (Cambridge, Mass.: MIT Press, 2000) (revised edition).

24. Robert B. Zoellick, "A Republican Foreign Policy," *Foreign Affairs* 79, no. 1 (January/February 2000): 63.

25. Inis L. Claude Jr., "The Balance of Power Revisited," *Review of International Studies* 15 (1989): 80.

26. *Straits Times*, January 22, 2001, 1.

Francis Kornegay, Chris Landsberg, and Steve McDonald

Participate in the African Renaissance

The United States reflects a triple heritage that has shaped societies throughout the Western Hemisphere. This heritage includes Native American, European, and African elements. These civilizations, however, have by no means equally shaped the foreign policy outlook of the United States and its relationships with the rest of the world. People of African origin in particular feel excluded from the U.S. foreign policy architecture. From an African perspective, therefore, an "ideal" United States would be one that considered its African heritage on par with its European legacy. Such a tradition would suggest that Africa should be defined as important enough to be regarded as "vital" to U.S. national interests. From this designation would flow a U.S. commitment to become a full-fledged partner in the African Renaissance, which is an ambitious bid for continental renewal reflected in a series of political and economic initiatives involving such major powers as South Africa, Nigeria, the Organization of African Unity (OAU), and other African partners.

Such a shift in policy focus would reflect the U.S. foreign affairs establishment's assimilation of the reality of a socially diverse and multicultural electoral constituency. Based on U.S. 2000 census data,

Francis Kornegay is senior research consultant with Linkages Development Agency, Chris Landsberg is lecturer in the Department of International Relations at the University of the Witswatersrand, and Steve McDonald is executive director of the Goals for Americans Foundation.

Copyright © 2001 by The Center for Strategic and International Studies and the Massachusetts Institute of Technology
The Washington Quarterly • 24:3 pp. 105–112.

What Does the World Want from America?

the white male electorate represents a demographically declining constituency in U.S. politics. Globally, a demographic shift is also underway toward an increasingly Afro–Asian world.

This demographic reality is one factor that has shaped an increasingly bipartisan approach to Africa over the last 15 years. The end of the Cold War and the effect of globalization on the U.S. economy and trade policy are others. In the past, U.S. Africa policy was the bailiwick of liberal Democrats and African American leadership. This situation no longer exists. Coalitions across party lines, including moderate Republicans, established U.S. sanctions against South Africa in the mid-1980s and, more recently, passed the African Growth and Opportunity Act. The photo finish to the U.S. 2000 elections, the even party distribution in Congress, and the perception that Africa is not of vital national interest makes a reasoned, nondivisive examination of U.S. policy feasible.

The point of departure for relations between the United States and Africa in the coming years should be based on initiatives that Africa's leadership is undertaking to control the continent's destiny, as embodied in the Millennium African Recovery/Renaissance Plan (MAP) spearheaded by South African president Thabo Mbeki, Nigerian president Olusegun Obasanjo, and Algerian president Abdelaziz Bouteflika. MAP's aim is to build foundations for stability by emphasizing conflict resolution; then to coordinate assistance to fragile African economies, employing a combination of debt relief, investment promotion, trade concessions, and foreign assistance with built-in African conditions by which Africa's leaders must abide. To support this millennium plan, what could the United States do to add more substance to the greater attention that it has recently paid to Africa?

Pivot on Fora

One of the mistakes that Washington's policy apparatus made previously was depending on a network of pivotal African states that proved untenable for U.S. political involvement, especially in Angola in the west, in the Congo in the heart of the continent, in Sudan with its "invisible war," and in Ethiopia and Eritrea. The United States must not rely solely on "pivotal states" and regional influences. Rather, it may want to concentrate on linking its key bilateral relationships involving some leading countries such as South Africa and Nigeria with its relationships with the continent's subregional groupings, such as the Southern African Development Community (SADC), the Economic Community of West African States (ECOWAS), and the Inter-Governmental Authority on Development (IGAD) in northeast Africa.

The model for such a strategy would be the recent combination of the U.S.–South African Bi-National Commission (BNC) with a regional U.S.–SADC Forum. The United States could expand such a forum beyond purely economic and trade issues to include a security and political dialogue. Alternatively, if the United States decides not to continue with the BNC framework, an expanded U.S.–SADC Forum, including a greater peace and security cooperation focus, should be seriously considered.[1] Either way, this interaction would provide an avenue for sustained communication aimed at resolving the conflicts plaguing SADC in Angola and the Democratic Republic of Congo. Similar forums, with the added emphasis on peace and security, could be established with ECOWAS in the west, IGAD in the northeast, and the East African Community (EAC).

Engaging Africa's subregional actors would not be a substitute for cultivating bilateral relationships with Nigeria and South Africa. On the other hand, if the United States also engages Africa's major regional entity—the OAU—and other subregional bodies, Nigeria and especially South Africa would not feel vulnerable to the charge of being superpower surrogates manipulated from Washington. Indeed, a key challenge of U.S. foreign policy toward Africa is allowing their foreign policy interlocutors sufficient freedom of maneuverability and not make them feel like mere pawns of Uncle Sam. This consideration is particularly important for South Africa as well as Nigeria, which are still navigating delicate transitions of democratic consolidation. Further, the development of such ties between the United States and South Africa and Nigeria must consider the insecurities of Africa's other powers and numerous smaller states.

This approach would be compatible with definitive moves the continent is making toward transforming the OAU into an African Union linked to an African Economic Community. In assessing the potential for such a framework, considering first the actual prospects of forging a U.S.–African partnership during a Bush administration with Secretary of State Colin Powell at the helm of U.S. foreign policy is essential. Little can be accomplished in U.S.–African economic relations unless security affairs are also improved.

It's Stability, Stupid!

Powell's anti-interventionist military doctrine is well known; his status as a U.S. hero, however, has not protected his military theory from scrutiny in Africa. How relevant are these critiques of Powell and the "Powell Doctrine" to a new U.S.–African relationship? Would a U.S. outlook based on the Powell Doctrine be an impediment to a workable U.S.–African partnership to promote Africa's peace and security? Or might this noninterventionist mindset offer an opportunity to define jointly a workable partnership that emphasizes African economic capacity? Africans prioritize the end of many conflicts destabilizing the continent as the necessary precondition for economic renewal. The key question remains whether a U.S. noninterventionist doctrine will help or hinder African security.

In an age of limited wars involving inter- and intrastate conflicts, the aversion to committing U.S. power in such situations is described by some commentators as reflecting a "hostility to limited war" even when such interventions may be the only means of decisively ending a conflict. According to Lawrence Kaplan, this belief reverses the Clausewitzian notion that political ends shape military means. As Powell is quoted, "We were able to constantly bring the political decisions back to what we do militarily."[2] Thus, the Persian Gulf War against Saddam Hussein is judged a military victory masking a political defeat resulting from the U.S. failure to crush the Republican Guard.[3]

In terms of U.S. Africa policy, this doctrine is blamed for the botched intervention in Somalia in pursuit of warlord general Mohamed Farah Aideed and for the ill-fated assault in Mogadishu, resulting in the traumatic scene of a bloody U.S. military corpse being dragged through the streets. This scene chilled what had promised to be an activist U.S. policy of engaging the United Nations (UN) on a range of peacekeeping initiatives, including developing the rapid reaction force. Such engagement might also have prevented the Rwandan genocide in 1994. All things considered, the legacy is a frightful tale of U.S. complicity in a string of UN peace operational failures in Africa. As the February 21–22, 2001, African regional workshop on the Brahimi Report on UN peace operations (held at Witwatersrand University in Johannesburg) showed, this dubious track record has resulted in some harsh African judgments about the UN's intentions to reform its role in conflict prevention, peacekeeping, and peace building. Assessments about the credibility of the support by the UN Security Council's five permanent members for peace operations in Africa were even more skeptical. As one experienced African general flatly stated, "The developed countries are not willing to enter into partnership with African countries to strengthen their capability for peacekeeping operations."

Indeed, the United States under the leadership of Powell, as the first American of African descent in that post, may have something to prove after all. Not only must he ensure that Africa is not marginalized, but also that the United States will undo a decidedly unheroic demonstration of recent U.S. reticence to engage in the continent's security affairs.

One can argue, however, that the unilateral anti-interventionist impulse may actually dovetail neatly with the emerging African peace and security agenda. The logical extension of the Powell Doctrine appears to favor U.S. assistance in strengthening both the UN's capacity to undertake a range of initiatives as well as indigenous regional and subregional peace operational capabilities in Africa. This strategy reflects an emerging African peace and security consensus. Autonomous but complementary peace operations capabilities could support a stronger UN peacekeeping capacity while promoting African peace initiatives. This

African peace and security consensus could well form the cornerstone of a U.S.–African peace and security partnership as an extension of the Powell Doctrine adapted to the needs of Africa. Although the United States is not interested in sending troops to far-off African countries about which the U.S. public knows little, Washington should ideally show its commitments through other means, such as helping with peace-keeping training in Africa or providing logistical support such as communications equipment, helicopters, and tanks.

The United States can also show Africa its support through its status as one of the five permanent members on the UN Security Council. The $525 million approved by the UN Security Council to carry out the Lukasa cease-fire agreement to end the war in central Africa is woefully inadequate. As perhaps the greatest challenge to Mbeki's African Renaissance, the conflict spans half the continent across Africa's middle, from Angola to the Sudan. Its widespread effects deserve greater worldwide attention, which can only be gained through U.S. support of, and cooperation with, regional actors.

Assuming that the United States can muster the political will, the political geography of U.S. influence in this vast inter-African region could prove to be a decisive factor bolstering African peace initiatives. The United States holds strong links to major state actors in the Great Lakes area and greater Central Africa, including close relations with Uganda and Rwanda. This influence extends to Angola, a key Kinshasa ally widely seen as mentoring, with Zimbabwean president Robert Mugabe, the successor government of Joseph Kabila within the framework of the Republic of Congo's defense pact. On the other hand, some vested U.S. interests may prove to be a complicating factor in pursuing greater Central African peace diplomacy. For example, official U.S. relationships are complemented by U.S. mining interests which concern many observers.

To make progress in this thicket of interlocking regional conflicts and vested interests, the United States will have to build on the close relations recently forged with South Africa. Although Pretoria has been careful to project SADC states such as Zambia as key facilitators in the

Congo peace process, South Africa has become an indispensable linch-pin in the fragile Lusaka peace accords. The United States' possible re-tention of the BNC as a vehicle of bilateral interaction between Washington and Pretoria is a positive sign.

Through a joint review within the BNC bilateral framework, pro-moting a U.S.–South African strategic partnership could serve an indis-pensable purpose as a confidence-building measure in maintaining U.S. engagement in the continent. Discarding the BNC would only rein-force the perception that unilateralism is an ever-present impulse driv-ing U.S. foreign relations. For the bilateral connection to work properly, Washington must be sensitive to Pretoria's need to not be seen as a sur-rogate doing the United States' bidding on the continent.

This lapse of sensitivity may have torpedoed South African and SADC participation in the African Crisis Response Initiative (ACRI), a U.S. policy response to the Rwandan genocidal fallout from the Somalia de-bacle. The $25 million per annum that the United States provided was less than what the Nigerian government spent per month during its military intervention in Sierra Leone.[4] This example typifies the funda-mental question of how much the United States is willing to invest in African peace and security capacity-building.

Can the United States, through the U.S.–SADC Forum, resurrect the ACRI in Southern Africa? In the view of some South African se-curity specialists, this action may constitute as much of a challenge for South and southern Africa as for the United States. The crux of African skepticism over UN peace operation reforms is a perceived lack of willingness on the part of developed countries to engage Af-rica in meaningful security partnerships. If, in fact, plans are afoot for the ACRI to devolve into a program for building a regional brigade capacity, could this maneuver not constitute the starting point of a U.S.–SADC security partnership compatible with an evolving division of labor between SADC, the OAU, and the UN? Otherwise, "African solutions for African problems" may devolve into little more than a roadmap for mutual disengagement between Africa and the United States, as well as other major powers.

The Global Challenge

What Pretoria might want to develop from a U.S.–SADC security dialogue is unclear. Certainly, Pretoria—as a means of safeguarding its own credibility with its neighbors—does not want to be perceived as a junior partner in a joint U.S.–South African hegemonic partnership within a southern African peace and security framework. Washington has a global agenda that looms much larger than its relations with South Africa and the African continent; Pretoria also has a global agenda to manage. Although the United States unavoidably occupies a major place on that agenda, Pretoria is not inclined to organize its global relations with the United States as the fulcrum. Therefore, Washington may have to opt increasingly for a greater multilateralization of its relations with Africa, particularly with regional fora as previously advocated.

Foreign and national security policy planners within the African National Congress government have not really articulated a comprehensive strategy, but the thrust of South African foreign policy is quite clear: cultivate an Africa-centered, south–south hemispheric alignment as a counterweight to the Euro–U.S. hegemony of the northern hemisphere, especially on the global economic front. South Africa's triumvirate with Nigeria and Algeria on behalf of MAP, for example, is complemented by a larger tri-continental alignment of South Africa, Nigeria, Egypt, Brazil, and India. The primary motivation is to mobilize a lobby of developing and newly industrializing countries in Africa, Asia, and Latin America behind the reform of the global trading system currently institutionalized in the World Trade Organization.

Washington may be well advised to begin taking Africa and its leading powers more seriously. North–South polarization is clearly not the intent behind Pretoria's southern strategy. Within this context, however, the global demographic future is essentially Afro–Asian (according to UN Population Fund projections), suggesting a world in which a fledgling African Union may potentially represent a more coherent actor on the world stage alongside the other major concentrations of humanity, China and India.

Will a hostile Afro–Asian countervailing bloc networked through the capitals of Pretoria, Abuja, Cairo, New Delhi, and Beijing emerge? Will an Africa led by South Africa and Nigeria carve out a role as a third party—a pivot, if you will—between the Atlantic powers and an unpredictable Asia–Pacific region anchored by such giants as China, India, and perhaps Russia? Certainly, if the United States and its Western partners do not begin to take Africa more seriously, then a less benign "G-8 of the South" may be inevitable. Whether such a G-8 could become an effective countervailing force to northern hegemony is another debate altogether. The onus is on Washington and the industrialized powers of the world to show good faith to relate to Africa.

The formation of a G-8 is not necessarily an idle consideration for the United States. Given that the United States is becoming less demographically Eurocentric with each passing decade, it will need to adjust its national security perspective to incorporate the emergence of Africa as an increasingly central fulcrum in a changing international system. In the current climate, dismissing Mbeki's African Renaissance and African Century as mere slogans of hope in search of reality is easy, but these global perspectives encompass Africa's ambition within the world at the dawn of the twenty-first century.

Notes

1. Simon Barber, "U.S.–SA Commission, a Clinton Creation, Has Bitten the Dust," *Business Day*, March 14, 2001, 2.

2. Lawrence F. Kaplan, "Yesterday's Man: Colin Powell's Out-of-Date Foreign Policy," *New Republic*, January 1 & 8, 2001, 18; John Barry and Evan Thomas, "Colin Powell: Behind the Myth," *Newsweek*, March 5, 2001, 10–14; Ellis Cose, "The American Dream in Living Color," *Newsweek*, March 5, 2001, 15.

3. Kaplan, "Yesterday's Man," 18. Though Kaplan infers Powell is to blame for this militarily victorious political defeat, some see this failure more broadly as a Bush administration political defeat.

4. The International Peace Academy (IPA)–based Nigerian scholar, Adekeye Adebajo, often reminds us of this fact pertaining to Nigeria's regional role in West Africa.

Mahmood Sariolghalam

Justice for All

From a cultural, political, and even economic perspective, Iran is not an isolated state. Although some may question the quality and scope of Iran's engagement with the external world, Iran and Iranians continue to play a role in diverse areas such as sports, movies, science, energy resources, international organizations, and Middle East politics. In national security, Iran clearly operates unilaterally and is isolated from others. The political consequences of Iran's security isolation are enormous for the country's internal politics, national economy, and foreign policy. Iran maintains no military or security pacts with any other state and relies on its own capabilities and calculations to defend the country and its political system. The security apparatus in Iran is highly endogenous and carries strong ideological convictions to maintain the political and the cultural sovereignty of the revolution and the state. Therefore, understanding the perceptions of the United States held by Iran's top security and political officials is paramount to comprehending Iranian foreign policy toward the United States. Because Iran is not a member of any Western security, or for that matter, political, club and because officials of the two countries do not communicate bilaterally,

Mahmood Sariolghalam is an associate professor at the School of Economics and Political Science of the Shahid Beheshti (National) University of Iran in Tehran and the editor of the English-language journal *Discourse: An Iranian Quarterly*.

Copyright © 2001 by The Center for Strategic and International Studies and the Massachusetts Institute of Technology
The Washington Quarterly • 24:3 pp. 113–125.

misperceptions and misguided analyses dominate policymaking in both capitals.

Most of Iran's top leadership is passionately attached to revolutionary ideals, to Islam as their guiding principle, and especially to the notion of "cultural sovereignty." This attachment is not confined to a few individuals. Rather, it is collective, institutional, and permanent, although concluding that revolutionary beliefs and practices have been seriously challenged during the presidency of Mohammad Khatami would be accurate. The revolutionary and nonrevolutionary definitions of Iran among equally powerful political groups are a reflection of the country's highly intricate identity crisis that has protracted Iranian national development. Over the last 150 years, conflicting views of Iranian national identity have led to incessant political instability and unrest. Despite galactic changes at the international level, all layers of Iranian culture and sources of identity have been able to sustain their conceptual potency, social constituency, and political relevance. The efforts of the Pahlavi dynasty to weaken the Islamic component of Iran's cultural structure proved highly unsuccessful. Similarly, the Islamic Republic's attempt to subordinate nationalist attributes to Islamic beliefs has been resented by the young and by the professional sector of Iranian society. History provides strong evidence of the permanence of both Islamic and nationalist dimensions of Iranian culture.

Although Arabs do not dissociate their Arab nationalism from their Islamic heritage, Iranians have so far failed to blend Islam and Iranian nationalism meaningfully into an institutionalized macrocultural system, whereby the majority of the country's citizens can form a basis of national identity. When attributes of Western culture are superimposed on Iran's nationalist and Islamic legacies, Iranians' identity faces serious conceptual and methodological challenges. The belief structure of an average Iranian carries three diverse and at times conflicting strands: Iranian, Islamic, and Western. In their active and reactive cultural behavior, Iranians pick and choose from the three layers, depending on the issue at hand. The political developments of Iran since Western entry into the country two centuries ago are a reflection of contradictory cultural trends and the unsuccessful attempts of political leaders to forge cultural consensus-building processes. The nature of the political system in contemporary Iranian history has vacillated, as various cultural groups have been able to highlight the cultural contradictions of rulers and reach power themselves. Iranian culture, in this respect, is a much more powerful force at the disposal of Iran's leadership than Iran's long-range Shahab-3 missile.

Whether nationalist or Islamic, justice is an important element of Iranian political culture. In international affairs, Iranians, like most Middle Easterners, are obsessed with it. Realpolitik is a much weaker political ideology than egalitarianism. There is a powerful belief that all countries are equal, no matter their size, gross national product (GNP), or level of military technology. Throughout the region, Islam provides individuals with a strong sense of self-respect and pride. Over the years, Israeli intellectuals have unsuccessfully tried to convince their leaders to remove checkpoints in Israel and start treating Palestinians politely. The same belief leads Iranian clerics to address the United States on an equal status, disregarding U.S. size, technology, power, and influence. The network of these cultural attributes provides a subtle yet robust foundation that shapes the internal and external politics of Iran.

Ironically, perceptions of the United States among Iranians in Iran are far more positive than other Arab perceptions of the United States. In contrast to a common argument in Washington, the most significant U.S. challenge in the Middle East may be to reshape its policies and to improve the U.S. image in the Arab world, not the normalization of U.S.–Iranian relations. From a geopolitical and historical perspective, the rift in Iran's relations with the West is temporary. The resumption of ties with the West in general and the United States in particular is the only viable option to make Iran a powerful regional country and improve the standards of living for Iranians. In its foreign policy formulations, no leadership, however strong, can act against geopolitical rationale and no force in Iran's foreign policy and national development is as potent as geopolitics. Iran's geopolitics and the realities of the political landscape within which Iran operates dictate a Western orientation in its foreign policy. In this context, the normalization of Iran's relations with the West is inevitable. Consequently, in viewing U.S. policy toward the Middle East, the importance of improving the U.S. image in the Arab world should not be underestimated.

During the last decade, Arab perceptions and views of the United States have sharply deteriorated. Two issues stand out: U.S. policy toward authoritarian Arab states and the "unjust" and "unfair" U.S. stance in the Israeli–Palestinian conflict. On the first topic, the level of distrust and apathy among Arabs toward the Arab political leadership is considerably high, and many Arabs hold the United States responsible for postponing democratization in the Arab world. On the second topic, since the establishment of the state of Israel, U.S. policy has been to keep Israel strong while applying diplomatic pressure on Tel Aviv to make compromises. The former policy has been pursued with greater vigor than the latter.

No U.S. administration has felt the urgency and the necessity to maintain a balance of power between Arab political and military power vis-à-vis Israel. The national security of key Arab states falls under the larger U.S. strategy in the Middle East. The Arab world, therefore, is incapable of exercising influence over Washington's Israel policy. Many in Washington may consider this problem an Arab, rather than a U.S., issue. Yet, the democratic roots of the United States and its deep sense of egalitarianism are notable for an attitudinal change toward the Arab polity. The resolution of the Arab–Israeli conflict ultimately rests on the concept of fairness.

Even the Palestinians have accepted the reality of the state of Israel; they and the Arabs seek only fairness. U.S. policymakers should not underestimate the conclusions of the common man in the streets of the Arab world. In the final analysis, what the average person thinks or feels may seem immaterial. But the key question remains, What is the nature of the foundation on which U.S. interactions with the peoples and states of the Middle East can be prolonged?

The United States should ideally provide some degree of psychological satisfaction to the disturbed but acquiescent millions throughout the Middle East. As a U.S. strategic thinker points out, "The American refusal to be bound by history and the insistence on the perpetual possibility for renewal confer a great dignity, even beauty, on the American way of life. ... But [America] must learn that equilibrium is a fundamental precondition for the pursuit of its historic goals. And these higher goals cannot be achieved by rhetoric or posturing."[1] Inattention to these foreign policy guidelines will not produce the necessary recognition, consensus, and respect for U.S. policies. More importantly, disregard for historical processes and insensitivity to the maintenance of balance among diverse players will not justify or internalize acceptance of a U.S. mediating role in the Middle East.

U.S. Challenges with Iran and Beyond

Based on the aforementioned cultural analysis, the United States must address a number of issues to move toward the inevitable rapprochement with Tehran. First and perhaps most importantly, the United States must conclude a realistic and objective analysis of the state and structure of power in Iran. Unequivocally, a deep philosophical distance exists between U.S. preferences for Iran and the realities of the Islamic Republic of Iran. Variations of religious thinking and norms will characterize Iran's political system into the foreseeable future. Some students in the early 1990s, who comprise the second generation of politicians and legislators in post-1997 Iran, are religious in a ritual sense but have a far less ideological orientation. Westernized sectors of the Iranian population, mostly in north Tehran and some urban neighborhoods, do not represent the whole country. Iran has its own Beverly Hills, but just as Beverly Hills does not reflect the whole United States, Iran's Westernized and secular classes are a minority.

From time to time I ask, "To what degree do the aspirations of my class, the intellectual community, represent the preferences of the Iranian population?" Most often, the answer is a resounding, "Very little." Most Iranians aspire to economic stability, the easing of ideological rigidities, and political freedom; smaller groups may pursue similar objectives in a different order. U.S. visitors to Iran should be cautioned not to confine themselves to luxurious receptions in north Tehran and conversations with a class that has a penchant for highbrow and pretentious living. They should seek out other social classes and people from rural areas. The overwhelming majority of Iranians pursue political, social, and economic reforms within the current political structure and through the electoral process under the current constitution. Almost no one is interested in another revolution or widespread chaotic circumstances; the young who account for half the population opt for peaceful and incremental change, in line with Iranian traditional cosmopolitan mentality.

In a Western sense, Iran will never be a secular state. Notwithstanding the fact that, after Israel, Iran has the most open political system in the Middle East, institutionalization of political pluralism and civil society will require much attitudinal change and economic restructuring.[2] Therefore, the current political system in Iran appears to have the resiliency to endure, with many modifications and reforms yet to come. The United States should play the role of an observer and avoid the temptation to get involved in Iran's internal politics. An interventionist policy on the part of Washington would only unite groups against an external enemy.

During the last two decades, an educated and nationalist class has arisen alongside the major holders of power throughout the Middle East. This class, mostly educated in the United States, has extensive exposure to the ideas of economic and political liberalization. This class ought to have a greater decisionmaking role in the transition from authoritarianism to liberalism. Whether authoritarian or liberal, Middle Eastern states need to interact with the United States. In a global context, no country can survive without a meaningful interaction with the Western world. The United States should prudently assist the gradual process of political change; the current focus on commerce and security is not adequate. Middle Easterners, whether Iranian, Arab, or Turkish, have a unique sensitivity to their sovereignty. A psychologically and culturally tailored approach will prove to be fundamental in the future role of the United States in the region.

The second area that the United States needs to reevaluate is the degree to which Washington should base its foreign policy, particularly toward Iran, on domestic politics and human rights conditions abroad. At least since 1979, political discourse in Iran has originated largely from within the political establishment. Even Khatami, an original member of the 1979 revolution, is now a symbol of a reform-minded class and revolutionary leadership. After the Iran–Iraq War, as the country began to engage in economic reconstruction, the academic community took the lead in setting a national agenda for political, philosophical, and social discussion. After eight years, from 1989 to 1997, of intense public debate on the course of the revolution, Khatami emerged as the insider to provide leadership for the new agenda. As Iranians debate the foundations of their identity and cultivate a more accountable state–society matrix, new faces, cleric and noncleric, will appear to lead the country. Given the richness of the debate and the involvement of the mass public, Iranians hope to frame a political system that reflects their multilayered identity. The process to achieve political stability may involve violence, similar to European and U.S. history in the nineteenth and twentieth centuries. In this process, religious reform is critical for Iran's political stability and continued cultural vitality.

Westerners may be able to provide methodologies in critical thinking but Iranians will mold the substance of reform, both religious and political. Most indicators show a great potential for inevitable, positive political change in Iran. Iranians enjoy resenting authority and, in doing so, they do not need the assistance of others to put their leaders straight. The United States should prudently not involve itself in the Iranian internal process of political reform and identity crisis resolution. Moreover, U.S. leaders should be circumspect in not taking sides in Iran's highly fractious politics. Some fall within the reform movement but oppose normalization with the West; similarly, some identify themselves with the conservative camp but favor gradual rapprochement with Europe and the United States. Individual views on Iran's U.S. policy are fluid, ill informed, and highly politicized. Even Khatami has remained reticent on normalization with the United States. The

United States should therefore focus on policies and interests rather than individuals and factions.

Despite more than two centuries of exposure to the West, Middle Eastern culture remains highly endogenous. Islam is a serious competitor to liberal thinking throughout the whole region. I remain skeptical on the plausibility and the applicability of the concept of "Islamic democracy." The overlap between these two political philosophies is narrow, and they originate from two different sets of assumptions. Perhaps they should not be compared because they stem from two distinct worldviews. Given the West's global hegemony, Muslims and Middle Easterners will have no viable option other than constructing frameworks and living in a simultaneous composite of Islamic, secular, and liberal tendencies, which often contradicts itself. Therefore, as the political thought of the twentieth-century Middle East proves, attempting to secularize Islam or to "Islamicize" liberalism is impractical. One must be careful in the unconditional application of Western concepts and frameworks to Middle Eastern structures. The most important challenge is to develop a political system that will deliver political stability, legitimacy, accountability, good governance, and rotation of power, while not disturbing religious thinking and cultural norms. The most effective role that the United States can play in this complicated process of change is to use its educational system to provide creative thinking and methodological innovation.

The third area of ideal change in U.S. policy, particularly toward Iran, is the significance placed on weapons of mass destruction and Iran's alleged attempt to "go nuclear." After 1979, for the first time in Iran's modern history, Iran's foreign policy behavior and national security doctrine were based on its own political structure and national priorities. Prior to the revolution, Iranian foreign policy behavior was founded on its international alliances. After the revolution, however, revolutionary ideology promoting Islamic sovereignty and the Iranian traditional quest for national independence set the basis for a new assertive foreign policy. From a national security perspective, Iran is an isolated country. To assure its security, Tehran has largely depended on its domestic resources. During the last two-and-a-half centuries, Iran has been victim to external invasion. Iran itself has no record of expansionism or invasion.

The paradox is here: Iran's intervention in the affairs of its volatile neighbors in the first decade of the revolution, an extension of its revolutionary credentials, is an aberration in its modern history. Iran's military capabilities are insufficient to address the potential threats from its neighbors. Therefore, the issue is not what Iran possesses or what Iran intends to do with its military potential. The real issue is that Iran is not a member of any military or security alliance. The United States would ideally encourage the Arab countries in the Persian Gulf to engage Iran in security discussions with the ultimate aim of forming alliances. Washington may even potentially participate as an observer in a security pact of Persian Gulf states.

Realists in Tehran understand that, unless the security considerations of small states in the Persian Gulf are addressed, political relations between Iran and other Arab countries will not thrive. The lack of security discussions between Iran and the United States only adds to the fears, misjudgments, and misperceptions on both sides. Washington needs to have greater understanding of Iran's security fears and then try to appease those fears by engaging Iran with regional countries and perhaps Great Britain.

Iran's military capabilities are not focused on Israel. Political rationality and restraint have been practiced in the post–Iran–Iraq War period especially. Iran's military and security leadership understand the consequences of its decisions and reactions. Defending the revolution and the state constitutes much of Iran's drive to maintain and upgrade its defensive potency. The perception in Tehran is that the ultimate U.S. aim is toppling the revolutionary state in Iran. Even the United States' willingness to talk with Iran is perceived as a strategy of disintegration through engagement. The disintegration of the Soviet Union is believed to be part of a U.S. plan, intensified after Mikhail Gorbachev's ascendancy to power, for the promotion of democracy, civil society, and economic privatization. Large numbers of individuals in Iran's military, security, and cultural establishments hold these beliefs. Washington needs to make a firm, uniform, and consistent decision on its security approach toward Iran: a policy of security cooperation with the current political system in Tehran or a policy of confrontation.

On a wider scale, U.S. security policy in the Middle East tends to place too much emphasis on threat perceptions. Given the urgency of economic, social, and educational issues throughout the region, even military solutions to the resolution of the Arab–Israeli conflict are becoming outdated. As a global power that is not alone in possessing military hardware, the United States has the responsibility to broaden the horizons of peoples and political leaders toward technological cooperation, political cohesion, and the rational reorientation of educational materials.

The fourth area of ideal change in U.S. policy involves adjustments in U.S. attitudes toward economic sanctions. Because of Iran's sensitivities to its national sovereignty, it is imperative that the United States take incremental steps to build up trust and assurances about its good intentions. As a great power with extensive interests in the Middle East, Washington should delineate a strategy toward Iran to shape appropriate perceptions through the next decade until the new generation comes to power and should not expect reciprocity from the current history-obsessed Iranian leadership. Removal of economic sanctions is a major step toward demonstrating U.S. goodwill. Americans need to understand how the Iranian political, administrative, and commercial systems function. The U.S. business community can serve as a neutral medium to change perceptions in both governmental bodies. No political impediments exist to economic and commercial cooperation between the United States and Iran.

Once U.S. oil and manufacturing companies set up their affiliates in Iran, they will have to work though the Iranian legal, legislative, and administrative systems. U.S. superiority in technology, organizational skills, managerial techniques, and decisionmaking expertise, as well as humble social culture, will then become apparent to those Iranians who have heard otherwise in the last two decades. In contrast, Americans will learn that Iranians are talented and cosmopolitan, with a capacity for grandeur. The United States will also learn that Iran is now differ-ent and not just another Middle Eastern country.

The United States also will have to work through a very complicated political and social system. The Shah's days when the consent of one person was adequate for the implementation of U.S. policies in Iran are over. Public opinion, diverse political groupings, and a robust legislative branch make Iran a unique country in an authoritarian Middle East. Therefore, the psychological and political ramifications of lifting sanc-tions will be far greater than the immediate economic benefits. Irrespec-tive of commercial motives, the United States should unconditionally enable companies to operate in Iran and transfer technology to Iran to change elite perceptions in the medium term. Engagement, subtlety, long-term perspective, and a deep understanding of the subject to be influenced were crucial in the continuity of British global power for more than two centuries. The United States cannot ignore these uni-versal laws of global grandeur.

U.S. leadership and decisionmaking bureaucracies need to use di-verse methods of engagement to enable the world to accept U.S. leader-ship and power. Much of the substance of accepting another's supremacy is psychological. Economic sanctions toward Iran, Iraq, or other coun-tries are considered attempts to achieve quick fixes to complex prob-lems. Simplicity, honesty, and straightforwardness in the United States have contributed to the flourishing of the world's most technologically advanced economy. But diplomacy and statesmanship are not business. With its great human and material resources, the United States must be the master of engagement not only in the Middle East but through-out the world. Diplomatic ambiguity should lead to results, not to stale-mate. Middle Easterners are very accommodating by nature. Even militant Islam is a reaction to frustration and not an intrinsic part of Islam. As a general guideline, not only for the political leadership in the region but also for Israel and the United States, a culturally conscious approach can win the soul of the average person in the Middle East.

The fifth area where the United States can play a new and effective role deals with changes in attitude. As mentioned previously, how individuals and states are treated tends to be much more important in Iran and the Middle East. The negative consequences of fingerprinting Iranian visitors upon arrival into the United States are greater than the personal grievances the same visitors may express regarding the U.S. role in the 1953 coup in Iran. Kindness, fairness, and generosity can achieve what reason, statistics, and arms cannot. This axiom can also be applied to the Israeli approach toward the Palestinians. British philosopher Isaiah Berlin alluded to the nature of the problem in the Middle East, pointing out that "the partly unconscious conviction born of experience [is] that virtue always loses and only toughness pays."[3] U.S. diplomacy does not incorporate cultural frameworks into its guidelines. The Europeans, in contrast, pay much more attention to the psychological consequences of the vocabulary they use. For example, the European Union uses "Iran's support for extremist groups" instead of the common U.S. usage of "terrorist groups."

To those who, by training, base international affairs on realistic assessments of power relationships, it may be unexpected to learn that Iran points to "American lack of sincerity" as a serious concern in Tehran's policy toward potential normalization. Sensing the logic of those who oppose normalization between the two countries is important. For example, one Iranian daily responded to then–Secretary of State Madeleine Albright's speech in March 2000 on U.S. policy toward Iran:

> How could Washington speak of Iran's "attempt" to become nuclear when Israel has possession of 200 atomic bombs? ... American officials constantly speak of the hostage taking in the beginning of the Iranian revolution, but they never explain to their people why ... this event happen[ed]? How could the [United States] complain of Iran's weapons of mass destruction when Washington itself holds the largest arsenal of weapons in the history of mankind? ... [The U.S.] secretary of state points out that the future of American–Iranian relations depends on improvements in Iranian behavior in judicial processes, minority rights, human rights, and terrorism. If this is the case, then much of humanity will be deprived of having relations with Washington. ... [The U.S.] secretary of state calls for freedom in Iran but forgets to mention that the Iranian people were deprived of freedom by the Shah who had the full support of the [U.S] government for 37 years.[4]

The political psychology that embodies these statements reflects a belief structure that seeks parity, fairness, consistency, and a judicious response. The author(s) of these statements probably know very little about the U.S. system. Moreover, they may not be equipped with the necessary international exposure to realize that international politics is not founded on charity or moral preaching. The author(s) are merely reacting to the contradictions in the behavior of a superpower from an internally generated political perspective.

Such authors and groups are increasingly influential. They cannot be denied the right to express their views since Iranian politics now, unlike many of its neighbors, has mass participation. Citizens from all over the country have an opportunity to enter politics and a chance to speak on issues about which they may know little. As societies experience more openness, active and organized minorities may possibly superimpose their views on silent majorities. Even in the United States, the largest democracy in the industrialized world, about one-third of the members of Congress do not have a passport and thus have not been exposed to the complexities and diversities of the rest of the world.[5]

Therefore, Washington is not faced with homogenous political machinery in Iran, unlike most countries in the Middle East. At times, political variation in Iran reaches a chaotic situation that frustrates those who want some degree of coherence to Iranian politics. Regaining the trust of the Iranian heart and mind requires a serious overhaul of U.S. attitudes toward Iranian national sovereignty, orthodox sectors of Iranian society, and the role of religious beliefs in Iranian politics. Greater U.S. sensitivity to the local cultural and political landscape in Iran can be demonstrated through the kind of vocabulary and political formulations employed by U.S. congressional and executive officials.

From a cultural perspective, the Middle East remains the most insular region in the world. Greater use of political psychology by the United States is necessary to alter the U.S. image throughout the Middle East. No industrialized country in the world is as generous as the United States in sharing its accomplishments with the rest of the world, and no other democracy practices as much tolerance for diversity as the United

States. It is prudent and logical then for the United States to project these and many other values to the rest of the world, provided that they are tailored to local cultural nuances. The United States is too well equipped to be misunderstood and to fail to create an equilibrium among diverse players.

Looking toward the Future

The aforementioned attitudinal suggestions are also valid for an arduous, ultimate coexistence of Israel with the rest of the Middle East. Israeli anti-Iranian pursuits are unnecessary. Iranian political culture must be considered in Israel's foreign policy formulations. Iran will remain an important component of the Middle Eastern power configurations. The utility of military hardware to produce political outcomes in the region is increasingly limited. Based on military criteria, isolated Iran should not have been able to defend its territorial integrity against an Iraq fully armed by Russia and Europe and generously financed by the Arab countries during the war. Yet, Iranians fought in the longest war of the twentieth century and, for the first time in their modern history, did not lose territory to an invader. In less than a decade, Iran will be a different and potentially much more dynamic and evolving state. The Israeli political machinery should not substitute short-term gains in publicity for potential mid- and long-term regional benefits. Iran has become an easy scapegoat for the endless difficulties in the Palestinian–Israeli negotiations. The United States has an important responsibility to differentiate between U.S. policy on Iran and the complexities in the Israeli–Palestinian peace talks. The current Iranian role in and contribution to the substance and outcome of the Israeli–Palestinian disputes is almost nonexistent.

Many elements make Iran an international country. Iran's energy resources, its geopolitics, and a basic Western orientation in its social and economic structure lead Tehran's foreign policy toward cooperating with great powers. For the current leadership in the Islamic republic, maintaining national sovereignty takes precedence over economic development. The order of these priorities will be altered only through changes in the new generation that will lead the country in the coming decade. A new worldly, cosmopolitan, and demanding generation will come to power through the electoral process to defend Iran's nationalist and Islamic identity. This generation will look beyond the Middle East to acquire Iran's national security and foster its economic development. U.S. policy toward Iran seeks quick results; they will not be delivered. The current attitude will only foster misperceptions and prolong unnecessary gaps. Normalization of relations between Iran and the United States is a means to an end and should not be the main U.S. objective in dealing with Iran. The United States has a far more important role to play and purpose to pursue, not only in Iran but throughout the whole region.

In less than a decade, new and young faces will lead the Middle East. The new leaders have no choice but to lead their countries to greater economic and political liberalization and gradually to abandon their authoritarian past. Religious and educational reforms top the agenda. The crucial element in this historic shift is political and methodical proximity to a West, and especially the United States, that appreciates and understands procedural and cultural nuances. The United States deserves to provide thought and leadership to the world but it need not advertise its desire to be hegemonic. U.S. bluntness about being the only leader in the world may not be psychologically wise. German behavior is an important example: as its power increases in Europe, its conscious humbleness also rises. As a U.S. strategic thinker said, "The scope of America's global hegemony is admittedly great but its depth is shallow, limited by both domestic and external restraints. America's hegemony involves the exercise of decisive influence but, unlike the empires of the past, not of direct control."[6] As a mid- to long-term U.S. strategy toward Iran and the Middle East, Washington needs to employ much greater subtlety in its multifaceted projection of power, especially at a time when new leaders exposed to mass politics are about to emerge.

Throughout the Middle East, the United States faces far more difficult challenges: changing the average person's mindset from a devastating subjectivity to an objective, more global, perspective; inventing a process and assisting regional political and social opinion leaders to move from destructive idealism to scientific realism; subordinating emotions and feelings to rationality and balance; meticulously engaging the region to make seismic shifts from authoritarian political culture to individualism and rational consensus-building processes; and cultivating private sectors that will take the lead in introducing rational social and political change in their societies. U.S. technology, innovation, and a resourceful educational system on the one hand, and a fair, balanced leadership that accounts for the local nuances in the Middle East on the other, will substantially reduce opposition to U.S. presence in the region. This course of action will also enhance its long-term image and add to U.S. credibility as a global power. This is the ideal United States.

Notes

1. Henry Kissinger, *Diplomacy* (New York: Simon & Schuster, 1994), 833.
2. Mahmood Sariolghalam, "Political Stability and Political Development: The Case of Iran," *Discourse: An Iranian Quarterly* 2, no. 1 (Summer 2000): 65–80.
3. Michael Ignatieff, *Isaiah Berlin: A Life* (London: Chatto and Windus, 1998), 182.
4. "A Review of U.S. Secretary of State's Assertions Regarding American–Iranian Relations," *Jumhori Eslami*, April 5, 2000, 11.
5. Moises Naim, "Clinton's Foreign Policy: A Victim of Globalization," *Foreign Policy*, no. 109 (Winter 1997–1998): 38.
6. Zbigniew Brzezinski, *The Grand Chessboard* (New York: Basic Books, 1997), 35.

Barry Rubin

What Is Right Is in U.S. Interests

Discussing what role the United States should play in the Middle East in an ideal world is difficult because the Middle East is probably further from an ideal world than any other region on the planet. Nevertheless, evaluating what has and has not worked—and examining some powerful myths about U.S. involvement in the area—helps show what a relatively optimal policy would be.

Fundamentally, the United States can best play a role in the region by properly pursuing its own interests, which are generally reasonable and basically beneficial to the Middle East. These broad interests include promoting a stable peace and avoiding war, rejecting extremism, fighting terrorism, encouraging democracy and human rights, helping allies, promoting economic development, and seeking to maintain a high level of U.S. influence. In an area where so many forces seek to promote war, instability, and violence, these goals are very relevant.

At the same time, however, doing the right thing—one might say, doing the necessary thing—does not make the United States popular. Ironically, in the Middle East many countries want the United States to behave as it currently does—and benefit from those policies themselves—

Barry Rubin is deputy director of the Begin-Sadat (BESA) Center for Strategic Studies in Israel and editor of the *Middle East Review of International Affairs* (MERIA).

Copyright © 2001 by The Center for Strategic and International Studies and the Massachusetts Institute of Technology
The Washington Quarterly • 24:3 pp. 127–134.

yet they seek domestic and regional gain by endlessly criticizing these U.S. policies.

To cite one of the most important examples of this system, Persian Gulf Arab monarchies enjoy U.S. protection from Iran and Iraq while often distancing themselves from U.S. policy stances. Egypt, the second-largest recipient of U.S. aid ($2 billion annually), usually attacks and rarely helps promote U.S. efforts in the Middle East, where trying, and often succeeding, to have one's cake and eat it too is a normal state of affairs.

The public reaction to U.S. policies should not be the yardstick for measuring these strategies' correctness or even the actual local attitudes toward them. Three anecdotes from Iran make this point. In 1946, a U.S. diplomat asked an Iranian newspaper editor why he always attacked U.S., and never Russian, policies. "The Russians kill people [who criticize them]," he responded. In other words, speaking ill of U.S. policy is safe and profitable while criticizing one's own government, that of other Arab states, or that of more vengeful foreigners is dangerous.

On the eve of the seizure of the U.S. embassy by Islamic militants after the 1979 revolution, the U.S. chief of mission wrote in an official dispatch that he had just finished a typical meeting with the new government's officials. They spent the first hour berating the United States and then asked for visas for their relatives.

Finally, a security officer who was held hostage told me that he concluded that the long lines of people waiting to visit the embassy convinced Iranian leaders that the bilateral relationship had to be destroyed, lest many of the revolt's key participants turn to the United States for help in gaining power for themselves. In short, to those in authority, the potential popularity of the United States—including its cultural invasion—is frightening.

Another example can be seen on the other side of the Gulf. For years, Kuwait and other Gulf monarchies harshly criticized the United States and said they opposed any U.S. involvement in the region. Yet, when the spillover of violence from the Iran–Iraq War threatened them in the late 1980s, they did not hesitate to ask the United States to put

U.S. flags on their oil tankers and then to protect them from Iraq when it invaded Kuwait in 1990. Once the crisis was over, however, and the United States had saved them, they reverted—publicly at least—to traditional attitudes. Nevertheless, they always know that the United States is waiting just over the horizon to rescue them again if the need arises.

Ideology might trump interests when rhetoric is involved, but this truism does not apply to the actual behavior inspired by power politics. Despite several decades of threats of anti-U.S. policies, often in response to U.S. support of Israel, those policies never came to fruition. When the Arab world—including the Palestinians—needed the United States as protector, helper, and mediator, these requirements always took priority over anti-U.S. rhetoric.

Equally important are the real roots of the most common and virulent criticism of the United States and its policies: that certain radical ideologies, countries, movements, and individual politicians revile the United States for trying to stop them from doing what they want. Such goals include uniting the entire region, or at least some other countries, under their own control; the expulsion of Western influence from the region so that their own authority can replace it; the systematic subversion of neighbors; the imposition of extremist systems; the destruction of Israel; and the use of violent strategies to seize power within countries.

Because the United States opposes the efforts of these states, regimes, and individuals, they demagogically portray the United States— as they carry out a propaganda war for their own interests—as being against "the Arabs" or Islam or self-determination, democracy, and human rights. Of course, blaming the United States allows many people to avoid taking responsibility themselves for their own mistakes and misdeeds, a common practice in other parts of the world but perhaps more widespread and superficially successful in the Middle East.

Having enemies, however, does not necessarily prove the United States guilty or represent any cause for shame. Extremist leaders like Ayatollah Ruhollah Khomeini, Saddam Hussein, Mu'ammar Qadhafi, Hafiz al-Asad and others were not expressing a misperception when they said they hated the United States. They knew what they wanted and were correct to see the United States as blocking their way. The United States was, and is, correct to stand in their way.

At the same time, the United States must necessarily ignore the siren song of those who do not wish it well. They promise to like the United States only if it lets them destroy Washington's real friends, and pledge to institute democracy and human rights if the United States just ignores their use of terrorism and repression. They ask for pity as victims after they have provoked the violence and crises that produce the very conditions from which they could have easily escaped.

Thus, an ideal situation is not one in which the United States accepts Iraqi domination of the Gulf, Iranian exportation of its own version of Islamic rule, Palestinian and Syrian rejection of a compromise peace with Israel, or other such activities. The best situation involves the United States effectively seeking a moderate and peaceful outcome and gaining sufficient support in the region for these endeavors.

A Look at the Past

In this context, U.S. policy and interests in the Middle East have done quite well during the last three or four decades, especially after accounting for the seriousness and the extent of the challenges faced there. Obviously, the list of miscalculations, misperceptions, and mistakes is long, including such notable events as the U.S. failure to foresee Iran's 1979 revolution, the 1990 invasion of Kuwait by Iraq, and the failure to bring down Iraqi president Saddam Hussein in 1991.

Nevertheless, the United States generally achieved its aims in the region. First and foremost, it stopped any expansion of Soviet influence. Even before the USSR's collapse, the United States had assumed the role of principal power in the region. In the Gulf, it helped maintain the area's stability and preserved the independence of the Arab monarchies. The United States was able to block either Iranian or Iraqi domination of the oil-rich subregion.

In addition, the United States helped preserve the stability and sovereignty of most of its allies in the face of huge domestic and regional efforts to overthrow them. It seized opportunities to mediate the Arab–Israeli conflict when possible. Oil prices rose and fell at various times, but access to petroleum was always maintained in a way that made continued economic development possible in much of the world.

No one should neglect such achievements while obsessing over shortcomings and errors. Perhaps the outcome of Middle East developments—at least inasmuch as the United States could have shaped them—was as beneficial as possible, given regional attitudes, problems, and conditions. Nor should U.S. policy be judged on the basis of exaggerated expectations. Just as Washington did not cause the area's conflicts, it cannot easily solve them. The United States could not end the Iran–Iraq War unilaterally and cannot end the Arab–Israeli conflict until the belligerents wish to do so.

Another important point in considering what might be the best possible U.S. policy is to remember that there was not nor will be any single ideal policy because situations constantly change, as demonstrated by the history of Gulf and Arab–Israeli issues. In the Gulf, the U.S. goal was preserving the independence of the Arab monarchies and preventing any radical force from seizing power in the area. In the 1970s, this policy resulted in U.S. support for Iran to counter Iraq's ambitions. In the 1980s, the strategy was to back Iraq's war effort against Iran's proclaimed desire to spread Islamic revolution. In the 1990s, the strategy involved direct U.S. involvement and dual containment of both Iran and Iraq.

Each of the transitions between these phases was badly handled. Still, the problem was not that the policy was inconsistent but that changing conditions required revised approaches. It is often glibly asserted that the dual containment strategy and sanctions have failed, but this statement is not true regardless of whether the effort is outdated today. Sanctions have greatly weakened a revival of Iraqi and Iranian military might and economic power, thus making them less threatening to their neighbors.

Similarly, regarding Arab–Israeli conflict issues, the United States has usually not created opportunities, but it has recognized them and tried to act productively to bring them to fruition. Among the waves of diplomatic effort were the shuttle activities of Secretary of State Henry Kissinger in the mid-1970s, the Camp David agreements brokered by President Jimmy Carter in the late 1970s, President Ronald Reagan's plan of the early 1980s, the Madrid peace conference organized by President George Bush's administration in 1991, and President Bill Clinton's high priority during his entire term on helping the peace process initiated by Israel and the Palestinians.

Highlighting specific U.S. misjudgments or, at the least, controversies raised over such decisions is easy. Still, U.S. efforts must be rated fairly highly as they played a central role in fashioning Egypt–Israel and Jordan–Israel peace treaties and helping to reduce the likelihood of war. Over time, the United States correctly learned that only those directly involved in the issue could make peace. The United States could help these efforts but could not guarantee success either by pressure or by some ingenious plan that dissolved all conflicts. This pattern also must prevail in the future. In the year 2000, the United States helped bring Israel and the Palestinians to the verge of an agreement, only to discover that the Palestinians were unwilling or unable, or both, to make any compromise deal.

Time has shown that strong U.S. support for Israel has been and remains a sensible policy. Israel is a democratic state that has been openly and consistently threatened with extinction by its neighbors. Israel's record of support for the United States is strong. Considering the radicalism and ambitions of several regional governments, Israel has been a bulwark against such activities both when the radicals were allied with the USSR and afterward, as they pursue their goals on their own.

The Lessons of the 1990s

In a sense, the 1990s were a laboratory for testing—and rejecting—the propositions most often advocated to alter U.S. Middle East policy sharply. To understand what the "best possible" U.S. strategy should be, one must closely study the lessons of this decade.

The United States' role and influence as the world's sole superpower was recognized and further consolidated in the Kuwait crisis. Thereafter, moderate Arab states continued efforts to maintain good relations with the United States and to use it as a protector, no matter how their public posture differed from that image. Syria tried to give the impression that it was cooperating with U.S. efforts to further the Arab–Israeli peace process. The Palestinian Liberation Organization, at least in its form as the Palestinian Authority (PA) governing the West Bank and Gaza, became a virtual U.S. client. After a long struggle involving U.S. sanctions, even Libya surrendered two intelligence agents for trial in the bombing of a U.S. airliner over Lockerbie, Scotland, in 1988.

Only Iraq remained openly defiant of the United States. Yet, although sanctions remained, Baghdad did not suffer greatly for its actions, for sanctions remained but were steadily weakened. The Gulf war coalition broke up, with France, Russia, and China leading the way in opposing the tough U.S. strategy on Iraq. The United States launched limited bombing raids, maintained no-fly zones, and preserved the Kurdish autonomous area in the north.

Most noticeable were the limits on U.S. power and influence that could be attributed either to mistaken U.S. policies or to the nature of the region, its problems, and its regimes. The United States was unable to press the PA or Syria into signing peace agreements with Israel, despite many Israeli offers of concessions on almost all key points. Equally, it could not keep some countries from breaking the sanctions on Iraq or the U.S.-imposed sanctions on Iran. The United States had very little success persuading other Arab states to move closer to peace with Israel, especially Saudi Arabia and Iran, even though it had protected both countries during the 1991 Iraqi crisis.

Although the Arab world frequently complains that the United States is a bully, the prevailing attitude seems to be ensuring that such a splendid bully is on one's own side. Moreover, there is ample reason to argue that U.S. failures occurred not because it was perceived as a bully but because it did not use its influence powerfully and effectively.

Why should various Arabs show gratitude to the United States as their protector and liberator when they did not have to do so in order to obtain the benefits? Indeed, the countervailing factors on this point were interesting. To indicate dependency on, and appreciation for, U.S. help would bring U.S. demands for reciprocal behavior. Moreover, in the context of their worldview, Arab leaders feared that the United States might seek to control the Gulf, or the Middle East in general, subordinating them in an imperial manner.

In short, although U.S. power was predominant and Gulf Arab states were ready to grant Washington a more important role than ever in protecting their security, the gains made by the United States during the decade fell far short of earlier expectations. The apparent lesson in the Arab world from the Kuwait crisis was that the United States could be more helpful, but the Gulf states could avoid paying much of a price for that assistance.

At the same time, Arab states in the Gulf are relatively less afraid of U.S. involvement and intervention than ever before. They are very much aware that the United States has been a source of arms and their protector, often exercising influence on their behalf. Consequently, despite all its problems—criticism and the undermining of sanctions against Iraq most obvious among them—U.S. Gulf policy, although requiring periodic adjustment, is probably about as good as can be expected.

An equally important lesson has been that attempts to make peace with militant states such as Iran, Iraq, and Syria have repeatedly failed. From the conciliatory policies of Carter that helped precipitate the Iran hostage crisis, to the efforts to prove U.S. friendship to Saddam Hussein before his invasion of Kuwait, through the humiliating visits of Secretary of State Warren Christopher to persuade Syria to join the peace process, to the disappointing campaign to persuade Yasir Arafat to conclude an agreement with Israel, U.S. flexibility has not persuaded the other side to act accordingly. For example, during the time that the United States tried to get Syria to make peace with Israel, U.S. policy never tried a systematic campaign of pressure on Syrian interests, including its occupation and control over Lebanon, to push Damascus in that direction.

This failure is extremely regrettable; a different outcome would be preferable. Nevertheless, such factors and experience must shape U.S. policy in the region. Whatever the specifics required, the United States must take a firm stand against radical states and movements. Too often, U.S. attempts to prove its good intentions and willingness to make concessions for this purpose have been interpreted as signs of exploitable weakness.

Israelis want a strong, successful U.S. policy in the region to ensure their survival. During the last decade, based on U.S. assurances, Israel has largely followed U.S. advice by taking risks and making concessions in the peace process with the Palestinians and Syrians. These risks are no mere abstractions but have helped lead to the deaths of dozens of Israelis, major security problems, and huge economic damage.

Now that this situation has blown up, they have a reasonable right to expect U.S. support in the resulting crisis. As before, the United States is the indispensable sponsor of peace negotiations, although progress can only be made if the Palestinians end the violence and show an interest in a realistic compromise solution.

The other vital issue for Israelis is U.S. deterrence of Iran and Iraq as they threaten Israel and seek to obtain missiles and nuclear weapons. Whatever the shape of sanctions against Iraq, they must be effective in slowing Baghdad's ability to rejuvenate its war-making capacity as much as possible. However the United States approaches Iran, its strategy should try to reduce the likelihood of an Iranian attack and its promotion of anti-Israel terror.

The situation is not simple, but then the Middle East is a very dangerous neighborhood and the world's most unsettled region. The basic problem is not some U.S. misperception or mistaken policy but the extremism and ambitions that make a protective U.S. stance so necessary. U.S. choices in the Middle East, as so often happens in foreign policy situations, must be predicated on the best conceivable choices with the knowledge that no perfect options or easy solutions exist.

Dmitri Trenin

Less Is More

The truth of that old adage, "Beware of what you wish for … it may come true," is coming home to roost in the towers of the Kremlin. Even before the long-delayed victory of George W. Bush, the councils of Russian president Vladimir Putin clearly and strongly preferred the Republicans. They hoped that the heirs of Reagan and Nixon, as good students of realpolitik, would "take Russia seriously;" treat it as a "normal great power," as they did back in the Soviet era; and forget all that nonsense of remaking Russia in America's image.

What is most troubling for Kremlinites since the arrival of the new U.S. foreign policy team is not the tough tone that the United States has taken toward Russia, but rather the symbolic and actual downgrade of Russia's importance on the U.S. government's list of priorities. Being seen as a problem is much easier for Russia to handle than being considered irrelevant or marginal. Far from having the potential to become "another America," it seems the Russian Federation won't even get the chance to be "another Soviet Union" in the eyes of U.S. policymakers.

The Russian ideal of the United States involves the United States treating Russia as a coequal. Nuclear strategic parity, achieved in the early 1970s, was emblematic of Soviet (and later Russian) elites' attitude toward, and expectations from, the United States. Following the

Dmitri Trenin is deputy director of the Carnegie Moscow Center.

Copyright © 2001 by The Center for Strategic and International Studies and the
Massachusetts Institute of Technology
The Washington Quarterly • 24:3 pp. 135–144.

demise of the USSR, the new Russian leadership genuinely hoped for a U.S.–Russian condominium. Bipolar conflict and confrontation would in their worldview be replaced by bipolar entente and engagement. The world's greatest and the world's newest democracies would jointly continue to manage the affairs of the world. Indeed, deep in their hearts, many members of Russia's old elites wanted to be the United States, or at least to be like the United States.

That this possibility was never realistic lies at the heart of the Russian elites' psychological problems with the United States. To continue along the same lines, however, is to miss the point: this fantasy is about the United States, not Russia. The dreams of a U.S.–Russian joint rule had barely been indulged before they were rudely dispelled. Indeed, after eight years, Russian policymakers and opinion leaders were growing heartily sick of the U.S. government's approach to their country. To the Russian political elite, suddenly nothing was right anymore about the approach of arguably the most Russophile Washington administration in history. The Russian critics' attitude could be summarized best by using the oft-repeated zinger of an early Soviet classic, *The Twelve Chairs* by Ilf and Petrov: "Don't teach me how to live my life, just help me out with money!" To their dismay, all the financial flows dried up after Russia's 1998 default.

Few, if any, illusions remain in the Russian collective mind about the United States. Perhaps, to paraphrase Lenin, we are at the point where we must "take one step back, in order to take two steps forward." At this juncture it may be helpful to think in positive terms of what Russo–U.S. engagement would ideally look like, from the Russian point of view. If Russians could be persuaded to draw up a wish list of what they would like the United States to do or (maybe more importantly) not to do, the results could well be summarized as below.

Great Power States with Privileges

Russia's assertive new leadership would highly value their country's full membership in the most exclusive club of world leaders, the G-8 forum.

For Putin, Russia's entry would be a badge of personal honor. Russia's leaders are painfully aware of their country's deficiencies and inadequacies and of the essentially political nature of an invitation to join the group as a full member. Moscow wants Washington, as an informal leader of the G-7, to take the lead in this endeavor. Until then, Moscow still wants their country to be treated as an equal member, on a par with the G-7 core.

Above all, the Russian political elite wants the United States to recognize Russia's importance, and treat Russia as a great power—not *in potentia*, but now. Because Moscow's brightest badge of international status is its permanent membership on the United Nations (UN) Security Council, this acknowledgement means recognizing the supreme authority of the Security Council in all matters of international peace and security. In particular, Russia wants the United States to abstain from any military intervention without first consulting the Security Council and obtaining its (i.e., Russia's) approval, effectively scrapping the 1999 provisions of the North Atlantic Treaty Organization (NATO) Strategic Concept regarding humanitarian interventions.

The corollary to craving recognition as an equal is that, almost without exception, Russians believe that the time for U.S. lectures on the merits of democracy, free markets, civil society, integration into the international community, and the like has come and gone. Ten years after the end of the Soviet Union, the general feeling is that the Russian Federation has come of age. Russians want Russia to be accepted as a functioning democracy, a market economy, and a member of the international community—with the important caveat that Russia "will be different" and must enjoy a "special status."

The majority of Russian elites hopes that the United States will stop trying to encourage Russian reform from within Russia. They want Washington to keep its distance. Above all, they want the United States to avoid picking favorites in Russian domestic politics and to let the Russians settle it among themselves. The vertiginous centralization of the political scene around the Kremlin since Putin's accession should make such agnosticism much easier for the United States

What Does the World Want from America?

today. The elite majority want the United States to remain uninvolved in the Kremlin–NTV dispute; to distance itself from the Chechen separatists; to stop second-guessing Russian military actions in the provinces; and to join Russia in the fight against the cresting wave of international terrorism, which threatens to engulf Russian and U.S. interests alike, particularly in the Caspian Basin and the greater Middle East.

Undoubtedly, a minority comprised of the liberal wing of the political elite—chiefly, the Yabloko faction in the Duma, NTV managers and journalists, and human rights activists—tenaciously holds the opposite view, that the United States must act to prevent Russia's slide toward what they see as a police state, as evidenced by, for example, curbs on media freedoms and violations of human rights, including in Chechnya. At the very least, they think, Kremlin leaders should be made aware of the international costs involved in taking these actions. These Russians seek to remind the Americans of the formula articulated by Andrei Sakharov, the Soviet Union's premier dissident: keep pressure on the authorities in Moscow, while helping Russia to transform itself.

The Mechanics of Dialogue

As with any state, characterizing a unitary Russian perspective toward the West is difficult. After all, a complex society with numerous interests seeks different outcomes from the West. Most business elites' wishes are realistic, but the realization of those wishes depends primarily on the success or failure of restructuring the domestic economy, consolidating an effective legal system, building appropriate infrastructure on a massive scale, and other such desiderata. Any Russian company's attitude toward the United States directly depends on whether they have managed to find a niche in Western markets or not.

Overall, the Russian business community wants the United States to be less protectionist and allow easier access to the U.S. market—everything from hard goods, such as metal and textile exports, to intangibles such as U.S. financial markets and the ability to establish Russian subsidiaries in the United States. They would be delighted by formal repudiation of Cold War economic legislation such as the Jackson–Vanik amendment, as well as of the remaining restrictions on high-technology exports to Russia. Regarding third-country markets for arms, space, and nuclear technology, the Russians would like the United States to agree with them on a mutual code of conduct or a division of spheres of influence.

The intellectuals, scientists, and academics who benefit from U.S. foundations' assistance programs, however, want their grants to continue. To many, these grants make the difference between continuing their research or abandoning it. For a number of Russian nongovernmental organizations, provincial universities, independent press centers, nascent labor unions, and so forth, private U.S. assistance is literally of vital importance. There can never be too much of it.

With U.S. funding comes U.S. options that can influence Russian society. Most Russians, especially the artists and intellectuals, are seriously concerned that the emerging image of post-Communist Russia in the West contains far too many negative stereotypes—kleptocracy, mafias, and neo-Sovietism. They wish that U.S. media and the entertainment industry were more nuanced and balanced in their treatment of things Russian.

Other interest groups have their own concerns that shade these national considerations. For example, for the Russian Orthodox Church, whose influence on state policies has been steadily growing since the collapse of communism, an ideal United States would not interfere in Russia's religious affairs. Noninterference means stopping the influx of proselytizing missionaries who are successfully recruiting members among the nominally atheist populations of Russia, Belarus, and Ukraine. The Orthodox Church also strongly objects to the invasion of U.S. popular culture, which threatens traditional Russian values.

As the one sector of today's Russia that looks forward to more, not less, of the United States, Russian civil society—slowly emerging from hibernation after the long Soviet winter—wants the United States to be supportive and helpful, but not paternalistic. Devising U.S. government programs to meet some of their needs is difficult; implementing them is even trickier. Private U.S. citizens and organizations, however, also have a very large role to play, helping that section of Russian society define its identity, get organized, empower itself, and consolidate the 10-year democratic and market transformation whose tantalizing promise still guides Russia's hopes and aspirations today.

Finally, among the more mundane but deeply felt issues, many ordinary Russians want U.S. consulates to be less stingy and bureaucratic about issuing visas to visit the United States. For the younger generation, the United States is a land of opportunity where they can get an education that will help them find a lucrative job or start a successful business enterprise. Although most of these young people want to visit the United States simply to experience the culture, relatively few aspire to settle down and become U.S. residents or citizens.

From the Kremlin's standpoint, an ideal U.S. foreign policy would involve high-level dialogue on all key issues. The Gore–Chernomyrdin commission served as a model for how the formal part of this dialogue could proceed; a host of private venues (such as the Aspen Institute strategy group, the U.S.–Russian business forum, or the annual world economic meetings in Davos) constitute the parallel nongovernmental channel. Ultimately, as discussed earlier, Russia's elites crave recognition as equals from their U.S. peers and still feel hampered by the lack of easy access to key figures in Washington as well as in U.S. business, military, and intellectual communities.

Economic Matters: Learning the Hard Way

Within the G-8 and outside it, the Russian government has by now learned some sharp lessons about the consequences of economic troubles in international relations. Payments on Russia's debts, which now exceed $150 billion, are becoming a progressively larger portion of the Russian federal budget. At current rates, the debt burden will rise from $3.7 billion in 2001 to nearly $18 billion in 2003, amounting to 80 percent of the federal budget. In 2000, Russia reached a debt restructuring/partial write-off agreement with the London Club of private creditors; it now wants the Paris Club of government lenders to follow suit. Even though the U.S. government is not Russia's principal creditor (Germany is), Russia would like Washington strongly to support easing Russian debt to help domestic reform.

Russia also wants the United States to provide support at the International Monetary Fund (IMF) and the World Bank for Russian initiatives. Throughout much of the 1990s until the 1998 financial collapse, the Russian government relied heavily on IMF loans. Moscow is now in the process of repaying those loans and does not want new ones, but it would like the IMF to provide a formal stamp of approval for the Russian government's economic policy, which in turn would ease Moscow's dealings with the Paris Club. Russia also wants the World Bank to expand aid for Russian infrastructure development, such as highway construction and the modernization of the country's vast and dilapidated railroad network.

For improvement in foreign trade, the key is Russia's accession to the World Trade Organization (WTO), which is a slow-moving process; Russia is unlikely to join the WTO during Putin's first term, which ends in 2004. Because Russian trade with the United States is only a fraction of Russian trade with the European Union (EU), the latter is likely to raise the most questions in the pre-accession talks. Pending accession, Russia wants the United States and the EU to drop antidumping practices regarding Russian exports such as steel and to open their markets to Russian goods.

The Russians want massive U.S. investment in their country and assistance with technological innovations. In their view, this support would provide the bilateral relationship with a critical mass of stability, as well as increase the U.S. stake in Russia's economic recovery and future prosperity. Still, many Russians are reluctant to give the United States access to some of the country's best assets, such as resources in the oil and gas industry or the financial sector, for fear of being sold out or simply overwhelmed.

Security Issues

At one time, global security and arms control were the backbone of U.S.–Soviet relations; they presently retain a high and troublesome profile. Moscow above all wants the United States to drop its plans for deploying a national missile defense (NMD) system. As an alternative, Moscow has proposed a global system to control missile launches, as well as a European "sub-strategic" missile defense system. The latter would result in joint threat assessment and decisionmaking, cooperation that the Russians have sought for a long time. As an added bonus, such a partnership would create an opportunity for technology transfers from the United States and would promote Russia's advanced air defense systems as the common shield against potential missile threats.

Budgetary requirements mean that Russia will have to continue reducing its strategic nuclear arsenal even in the absence of a third formal Strategic Arms Reduction Treaty. Nevertheless, Russia wants the United States to agree to even lower common weapons ceilings. Washington would ideally abide by a limit of about 1,000 weapons on each side while committing itself to continue observing the 1972 Anti-Ballistic Missile Treaty. First and foremost, Russia wants the United States to keep the system of strategic arms control alive and to reinvigorate it by involving other nuclear powers.

Russia's desire for the United States to stop further NATO expansion, especially into former Soviet territory, is well known. The Russians are not fond of a continued U.S. military presence in Europe and would shed no tears if U.S. forces departed the continent altogether. For Russia, Europe without a U.S. military presence is a much friendlier and perhaps more tractable neighbor.

At the same time, Moscow wants U.S recognition of Russian vital security interests across the entire post-Soviet space, including the three Baltic republics. Despite its recent travails over Chechnya, Russia sees the Organization for Security and Cooperation in Europe (OSCE) as its favorite regional security organization in Europe and wants the organization's role strengthened. For a long time, Moscow has wanted the OSCE to be modeled on the UN, complete with its own Security Council, with Russia as a permanent member. Ideally, the OSCE, having triumphed over NATO, would serve as a meeting point for Russia, the United States, and the EU in an effort to build a trilateral security arrangement. Such an OSCE, in Moscow's view, would need to adjust its current "geographical slant" and monitor the security situation in Europe's west as well as its east.

In the Balkans, the Russians would like the United States to enhance the UN role in Bosnia–Herzegovina and Kosovo to the point of embedding the NATO-led operations within a UN context. In Kosovo, southern Serbia, and Macedonia, Moscow wants Washington to be more proactive about addressing the danger of ethnic Albanian nationalism. Throughout the region, the Russians want to be party to joint decisionmaking.

In the former Soviet states, Moscow wants the United States to lower its political and security profile. U.S. attempts to enhance geopolitical pluralism through association with Georgia, Ukraine, Uzbekistan, Azerbaijan, and Moldavia are viewed as inherently anti-Russian. In the Caspian region, Moscow wants the United States to be less concerned with the figment of Russian neo-imperialism and to drop its attempts to reroute pipelines away from Russian territory. Russia also frowns upon participation of even small U.S. military contingents in joint Caucasus exercises with former Soviet forces, as well as grants to their nascent military establishments, if only because of the potential loss of arms markets.

Arms sales are a major bone of contention. The Soviet Union had a predominantly military economy with a small civilian sector. Perestroika raised global expectations that Moscow could convert its mammoth defense industry to civilian uses. Conversion failed. Another Russian daydream, however, followed: the dramatic expansion of Russian arms sales to new, paying customers across the former Cold War divide.

Yet, in the world arms bazaar, the Russians feel they have fallen victim to grossly unfair competition from the United States, which has constricted Moscow's market to the Asian "ghetto" of China, India, and Iran. Russia wants the United States not to interfere with Russian expansion into the lucrative markets of the Persian Gulf, Turkey, and the new NATO countries of central Europe. Better yet, Russians would welcome U.S. offers to coproduce weapons systems. From the Russian point of view, this possibility is not entirely fanciful: elements of the former Soviet space industry, such as Energiya Corporation, which have actually been cooperating closely and profitably with their U.S. counterparts, are enthusiastic advocates of U.S.–Russian cooperation. Should such a venture ever become a reality, the attitude of the Russian military–industrial complex toward the United States would improve dramatically.

Other than arms sellers, the Russian nuclear power ministry, Minatom, which is in fact a major state-owned corporation, is the entity with the most significant network of interests abroad. Minatom wants the United States to stop excluding it from the newly industrialized countries. It deeply resented the U.S. refusal to incorporate Russia into the Korea Energy Development Organization (KEDO), which led to North Korea's Soviet-made reactors being replaced with U.S. ones. The double standard was exposed, in Minatom's opinion, when the United States loudly protested against Russian deliveries of similar technology to another problem country, Iran.

Regional Flashpoints

The Russians, in the back of their minds, see the United States as the ultimate long-term guarantors of the territorial status quo in northeast Asia, including Russia's own Far Eastern provinces and Siberia. Indeed, East Asia provides Russia with far fewer reasons to complain about U.S. behavior than the European scene. Moscow wants Washington to proceed slowly on theater missile defense plans (as well as on NMD) mainly because it fears an accelerated initiative would provoke China to expand its nuclear and missile programs and embark on a rearmament drive, allowing Beijing to reach strategic parity with Moscow within the next 10–15 years. Russia would prefer the United States remain militarily involved in Asia while not provoking the Chinese. An armed conflict between China and the United States over Taiwan would put Moscow in an impossible dilemma. From the Russian point of view, few things could be more dangerous.

In the greater Middle East, Russia aspires to an important role. It wants the United States to respect its status as a peace cosponsor in the Israeli–Palestinian dispute, while recognizing Moscow's views on Iraq. The problem with the former issue is that Moscow has little to offer either side in the conflict and its current lack of influence reflects this shortcoming. As for Iraq, Russia secretly rejoices at the U.S. continuation of the sanctions regime because it contributes to higher oil prices. Moreover, U.S. air strikes against Iraq allow Russia to step forward as a friend of the Iraqi people and thus to hope for special favors from Baghdad once sanctions are eased or lifted.

The Russians would like to collaborate with the United States in the struggle against the threat of international terrorism, especially in Chechnya, Central Asia, and Afghanistan. Russia's southern flank is exposed and vulnerable and is regarded as a source of clear and present danger by Moscow. Many Russians, however, still suspect the United States of engaging in foul play in this area, surreptitiously encouraging Chechen separatists to undermine Russia's residual influence in Central Asia and the Caucasus.

Overall, Russia's wishful thinking about the United States is a microcosm of the current state of Russia itself. The views held by the political elites are highly defensive. As was once famously said of the British, the Russians have lost an empire (indeed, much more) but not yet found a role. For the most part, Russia's wish list is negative: the United States should leave Russia to its own devices; abandon activism such as NATO enlargement, Kosovo intervention, or NMD deployment; and recognize the Russian sphere of influence in former Soviet space. Interest in Russo–U.S. engagement, however, has grown dramatically weaker. Moscow is not ready and has no political will for a long and arduous westward pilgrimage.

Michael Stürmer

Balance from Beyond the Sea

W hat kind of a world does the United States wish to have? People in Washington ask that question continuously. The answer has always been, instinctively, that the best of all possible worlds would be one that resembles God's own country. On close inspection, however, a world full of Americas and Americans would detract from the uniqueness of the United States. The world would also have plenty of strong egos, full-throttle consumption, and an excess of Manifest Destiny—perhaps somewhat less than paradise-on-Earth. U.S. narcissism has always been coupled with incredulity over the existence of countries that do not wish to be like the United States.

With the arrival of a new administration in Washington's hallowed halls, the rest of the world asks more pertinent questions: what U.S. policies are desirable and how can the world affect them? Because Washington habitually does not pay excessive attention to non-U.S. desires anyway, contradictory and self-serving as they must surely be, the chances of their wishes being granted may be as unlikely as finding a genie in a bottle. For, inside the Beltway, there are no genies, and beyond the shores of North America, there are not too many deserving recipients of three wishes. Nevertheless, formulating reasonable expectations may

Michael Stürmer is a professor of history at Friedrich-Alexander University in Erlangen-Nuremberg, Germany, and is chief correspondent for *Die Welt*.

Copyright © 2001 by The Center for Strategic and International Studies and the Massachusetts Institute of Technology
The Washington Quarterly • 24:3 pp. 145–153.

be more than just another exercise in academic futility, as it helps iden-tify roles and responsibilities between the United States and other coun-tries, those that are friendlier as well as more dependent.

Present at the Creation

Germany has been lucky; the genie granted most of its wishes about the United States. Germany is, and has been for the best part of the last five decades, the focus of U.S. attention on the European continent. Germany was the chief prize of the Cold War since the first Berlin crisis in 1948–1949, the locus of Intermediate-Range Nuclear Force (INF) deployment from 1979 to 1987, a reluctant "partner in leadership" (Bush *pere*) in 1989, the economic heavyweight among the European Union (EU), and the central country for the North Atlantic Treaty Organization's (NATO) stabilizing role in Europe and beyond.

For a united Germany, even more than for the divided Germany of the Cold War, the United States' most important function is as the bal-ancer from beyond the sea—not only in terms of residual Russian nuclear potential but, even more important, in terms of the collective psyche of European countries. With the United States continuing to be a "Euro-pean power," as Richard Holbrooke has stated, all the imbalances, un-certainties, and nightmares of Europe are manageable. Without the United States, the ghosts from the past would unpleasantly appear, en-hanced by the fact that Germany is, by far, the largest economic player in Europe.

Today's Europe did not invent itself out of enlightened self-interest after the catastrophies of, as French president-in-exile Charles de Gaulle proclaimed in 1944, "la guerre de trente ans de notre siecle" (the thirty-years war of our century). Europe was created by the en-lightened self-interest of the United States, a process that did not begin with NATO in 1949 but with the decision for "Europe first" in 1941. The creation continued at Bretton Woods in the fall of 1944, when the United States designed a global economic system based on the strength of the U.S. economy and the U.S. dollar. At a fixed exchange rate to bullion gold, U.S. currency became the anchor for the devastated currencies of Europe, including the deutschmark introduced in 1948. This grand design combined immediate U.S. interests with broader global interests. The International Monetary Fund (IMF) was set up, together with the World Bank. The Organization for European Economic Cooperation was designed to coordinate the rebuilding of liberal economies throughout Europe. In 1998, Josef Joffe identified the rationale of the U.S. role with the principle that "great powers remain great if they promote their own interests by serving those of others."

After 1945, though, one-half of the world was reluctant to follow U.S. leadership, indeed, was openly hostile to the pillars of U.S. power, liberal democracy, and free enterprise. This situation led not to the investment of less energy in the *Pax Americana*, but to the employment of more material and manpower to meet an "implacable challenge," as George Kennan wrote. Under the glacial spell of the Cold War, the United Nations (UN) did not deliver a better League of Nations as intended by the luminaries of U.S. idealism. So the United States under President Harry S. Truman set out to counter the Soviet land empire with a far-flung sea alliance centered on the continental United States, the Pacific Rim, and Western Europe.

The Truman doctrine of 1947 was a defining element in founding the future *Pax Americana*. It rallied "the West" behind the Stars and Stripes against the forces of totalitarianism, past and present. The Germans—at least those happy enough to be on the Western side of the national debacle—suddenly and unexpectedly found themselves in the victors' camp. Based on this assumption, Konrad Adenauer, first chancellor of postwar Germany, built his grand design of "Westintegration" now, national reunification later. For the Federal Republic of Germany and the process of Western European integration, the United States was indeed, as Dean Acheson chose as the title of his memoirs, "Present at the Creation."

Never was the United States' grand design more decisively translated into action than through the North Atlantic Treaty and, subsequently, through NATO and the deployment of U.S. combat troops and nuclear weapons in Europe. British and Canadian efforts had helped to convince the Truman administration that the combination of the Marshall Plan (1947) and the Brussels Pact among the Western European states (1948) was not enough and that Soviet expansionism throughout the world needed a more comprehensive European response. The United States was willing to lend its support to the Western Europeans and bolster their defenses, but Europe also would have to make a decisive contribution.

Germany and Japan were defeated but still potentially great powers; the Soviets might make them an offer impossible to refuse, strategically defeating the West. To avoid this situation, the Western Europeans set up a system of economic cooperation and integration to include Germany. In return, the United States, with its nuclear arsenal, would offer military protection. In his memoirs, Truman unsentimentally explained that, without the territory between the Rhine and the Elbe rivers, the defense of Western Europe would be "nothing but a rearguard action on the shores of the Atlantic Ocean."

What Truman offered was a kind of double containment: containing Stalin's presence and Hitler's past—the reality of the "Soviet Threat," as the Pentagon would call its annual review, and the trauma of German domination. The Federal Republic of Germany was established in 1949, the German chancellor renounced weapons of mass destruction in 1954, Germany assumed a form of sovereignty in 1955, and German forces then entered the fold of NATO.

More importantly, the exchange rate of the U.S. dollar to the German mark was fixed at a level that allowed Americans to invest generously and cheaply in West German industries. Because the Germans could outperform not only European but also U.S. competitors in classic industrial goods, for which the postwar world had an insatiable appetite, Germany sold them duty-free within the fast-emerging European Economic Community (EEC). On top of all those blessings came, for the first time in history, an ample supply of energy through cheap oil, courtesy of the United States. Truman's "grand design," as he had called it, came true. When, 10 years after NATO's founding, the Soviets approached nuclear and missile parity with the United States, they faced a double-layered Western alliance: NATO on the outside, the EEC on the inside.

The Europeans tried to maintain some independence from the United States. Great Britain and France, after their Suez debacle in 1956, opted for national nuclear deterrents, not to equal the mighty Soviet Union, but to have some political leverage with the United States. When de Gaulle evicted NATO from its elegant quarters at Fontainebleau in 1966, he was trying to avenge the humiliation of having been rescued during the war by "les Anglosaxons," and of the United States' success at rebuilding Western Europe's security and prosperity. The German response was first the antinuclear movement, in blissful ignorance of the peacekeeping function of nuclear weapons; then the massive and prolonged protests against the Vietnam War; and finally the peace movement in the wake of the INF standoff between the Soviets and NATO. The rebellion against Adenauer's patriarchal rule and the rejection of U.S. moral superiority combined with sharp generational conflict and the fear of becoming a nuclear battlefield. The United States, or rather the image of the United States, provided a catalyst for controversy among the Germans: sons against fathers, left against right, dreamers against realists.

Meanwhile, the United States continued to build vast arsenals of nuclear weapons and, almost in parallel, a sophisticated cathedral of strategic arms control. After the Berlin crisis of 1961 and the Cuban missile crisis of 1962, the United States and the Soviet Union entered into a silent alliance to avoid being drawn into direct confrontation, over Germany or other issues.

By and large, evolution was slow, and the established balances in Europe's Cold War lasted until the night of November 9, 1989. The subsequent unraveling of first the German Democratic Republic and then the Soviet empire became a still-ongoing test for the United States and its European partners. In the defining moment following the fall of the Berlin Wall, the United States was, once again, present at the creation. Strong U.S. interests in being a "European Power"—instead of just a power in Europe—and having easy access to northern Africa, the Middle East, and Central Asia proved to be a leitmotif of U.S. policy.

Out of Europe's Area

Only in the vaguest terms did the NATO allies in their 1991 strategic guidelines agree that security of vital resources and freedom of the strategic sea lanes were common concerns. NATO planners and European defense ministers knew that they would be asking for trouble if they were more specific or even mentioned the Middle East by name. Apart from the Balkans, the eastern shores of the Mediterranean to the Persian Gulf and beyond are the most likely places from where threats to Europe's well-being might emanate. Although these areas are clearly far beyond the wildest fantasies of any European Security and Defense Policy (ESDP) enthusiast, NATO too has not much of a policy beyond Turkey. Even on Turkey's long-term future, its partners have found little agreement. Although Washington sees Turkey as the strategic centerpiece among Europe, Asia, and Africa, Europe feels that accepting Turkey into the EU is beyond a reasonable expectation because Ankara does not have much to offer in return. The Turks, meanwhile, retaliate by making the birth of ESDP as difficult as they can, and the Europeans carry their frustration to Washington—without much avail.

In the Middle East, the Europeans have not been willing or able to play any part except that of paymaster general for the Palestinians and of purveyor of much unsolicited advice—in many divergent directions—to all sides. The United States, busy micromanaging an elusive peace, has not been ready to invite the Europeans to take a more proactive part either. Officials in European capitals believe that only the United States can balance all the dangerous imbalances of the Middle East—but this assessment is linked to a free-rider mentality. The moment of truth is bound to occur when the United States faces more than one major crisis at a time. Except for the United Kingdom, which still shares the burden of policing the no-fly zones over Iraq, no European country has come forward to offer more than commentary on how to do things better. France has all but hindered the U.S.–UK action through its position in the UN Security Council. Germany tried, with respect to Iran, to play the good cop–bad cop game. Now, with a new U.S. administration that cares more about oil, gas, and pipelines than past humiliations and the human rights record of the ayatollahs, the Europeans would be well advised not to be surprised by an announcement out of Washington and Tehran, one day soon, that the past is the past and the future is the future. Iran, after all, needs industrial equipment on a vast scale. An entire reassessment of Iran's ability to diversify its economy beyond oil revenues will eventually occur, and the Europeans will want to take part.

In the Far East, Europeans tend to close their eyes and think of business. The strategic equation is left to the United States: the nonproliferation agenda, the reassurance of Japan under the shadow of its giant neighbor, North Korea's grim regime, or the Middle Kingdom itself. The Europeans still have to learn that the great seismic shifts of the twenty-first century and, by a natural consequence, the great conflicts of the future will take place in Asia, and that the United States faces more than one implacable and inescapable challenge east of the Suez and west of Alaska. Sooner or later, the United States will expect more than applause or criticism from the spectators' ranks. The very minimum will be a circumspect EU trade and investment policy. As the EU machine, however, does not habitually look at economic issues in an overall political and strategic context, governments will have to be aware of the potential for Atlantic discord—and preempt it in time. What Europeans in turn could and should expect is that Washington will not use its enormous leverage to create favorable conditions for U.S. companies alone—as so often happens in the Arab world when U.S. companies and their envoys hint at the link between U.S. goodwill and U.S. business.

The New Face of NATO

Ultimately, the key question for the Europeans is, Will the United States continue to play two roles, both as balancer from beyond the sea and strategic lender of last resort? After the "Two-plus-Four" process delivered a united Germany into NATO and the EU, the London *Economist* had a cover featuring an American GI leaning out of a train window with a European girl outside the train saying to the GI, "Nice meeting you." This farewell has thus far not materialized. Both sides are driven by what de Gaulle used to call "la force des choses": the Europeans become more European, and the Americans become more American. The first Clinton administration assumed office with the somewhat less than inspiring slogan, "It's the economy, stupid," but it experienced a steep learning curve, not only in the Far East and with the unholy strife in the Holy Land but also with Europe. The second Clinton administration coined slogans and policies such as "selective engagement"—which concerned the Europeans—and "assertive multilateralism"—which also was not very reassuring. Winston Churchill, Britain's wartime premier, once remarked in his caustic way that you could always rely on the Americans to come up with the best possible solution "after they have tried all others." The wars of the Yugoslav secession saw this premise in action—from U.S. unilateralism to the Dayton agreement, the successful conclusion of the air war over Kosovo, and Milosevic's demise.

Relations with Russia and the enlargement of NATO, although intimately connected, have been treated separately. U.S. leadership has been strong, indeed single-minded, ever since Clinton said in 1994 that it was not "if but only when" the countries coming in from the cold would be welcomed into the bosom of NATO.

The Europeans, invested intellectually and politically in NATO's "Partnership for Peace" program and concerned with Russian anger and revenge, followed with notable reluctance, except for the German defense ministry under Volker Rühe, advised by the RAND Corporation. The great majority of Europeans accepted that inviting the countries east of the Oder river into NATO was politically desirable and, indeed, that keeping them excluded was almost immoral. Only the first three countries—Poland, the Czech Republic, and Hungary—would pose no major accession problems; the difficult part, however, would follow the decision about the future of the Baltic states. Excluding them from NATO membership, on which their governments banked, would mean

honoring Russia's imperial instincts and subscribing to Moscow's geopolitics of the "near abroad." Including them in NATO's fold, by contrast, would mean expanding NATO to the gates of St. Petersburg and
severely testing relations with Russia.

No Russian, reformer or not, ever failed to say that the second part
of NATO's enlargement would awaken the worst in Russian domestic
affairs and that Russia would not soon forgive the West. When NATO
embarked on the enlargement voyage, NATO–Russian relations were
on an even keel, and the NATO–Russia Council looked, to the Russians at least, like a serious place to sort out differences. Instead, it
turned out to be a place where NATO lectured the Russians. The Russians were not amused. Since then, anger over the Kosovo war has been
overcome, but the Brussels-based Council and the Founding Act are
hardly a solid foundation for settling the more divisive issues on NATO's
agenda—or, for that matter, the more recent U.S agenda.

Europeans who failed to seriously consider the wider consequences
of NATO enlargement during the past decade are now faced with a dilemma that is neither for the United States nor for the Europeans to
solve. The United States has remembered that it is a maritime power;
that Asia is the great stage for the dramas of the twenty-first century;
and that it has other, more vital conflicts to settle with Russia (nonproliferation, conflict with radical Islam, cooperation against drug trafficking, and large-scale, state-sponsored terrorism). Moreover, the more
the hegemonic struggle with the Middle Kingdom looms over the Pacific, the more Washington will cherish long-term strategic stability, indeed partnership, with the Russians. The Europeans, being much closer
to the bear's den, may feel caught in the middle. Foregoing enlargement is impossible but whatever NATO does will carry a high price.
NATO's partners must address the problem not only as a regional issue
but also in its global context.

NATO has always been a maritime alliance, with the organizing
principle the erstwhile Soviet threat and, less obviously, the territory's
defense from the open seas. The more NATO moves, politically and
militarily, away from the shores and into the heartland of Europe, the

more likely that one day, if something goes wrong, Neville Chamberlain's dismissive words of 1938 about "faraway countries of which we know nothing" will be echoed.

NATO has not strengthened its military defenses since the Red Army left its garrisons in Central Europe; the Europeans have not made much of an effort to face the challenges of global instability and insecurity. Without having prepared the analytical and diplomatic groundwork, the Europeans embarked on ESDP in 1999 as an answer to their uncertainties and even frustrations over U.S. policies in the Balkans and U.S. unilateralism. Even the Clinton administration, generally well disposed toward the European venture, did not hide its misgivings about a "virtual force," as U.S. secretary of defense William Cohen called it, about "ganging up," and about the individual military budgets that did not even match NATO commitments and were hardly sufficient to support a European force. Individual Europeans or Europe as a whole have not answered most of the questions the Americans—continuing to be the strategic lender of last resort—are entitled to ask. Above all, the proclaimed goals of ESDP are far beyond the political concept guiding any future deployment. There are hardly any strategic guidelines consistent with the NATO model and compatible with NATO theory and practice.

This transatlantic nondialogue is not made easier by the new administration, after mighty pronouncements during the election campaign, now investing massive political capital in national missile defense (NMD) and allocating it vast resources without bothering to inform or consult the European allies. So far, most or all of the European allies had been hoping that, due to unsatisfactory technical tests, the NMD problem would just go away. Clearly, the Clinton administration in its parting days was not too keen to make any firm commitment on the issue. The Bush administration has toned down its early enthusiasm but leaves no doubt that it will press ahead. The United States will not soon convert the Europeans to the gospel of NMD; instead, they will do whatever they can to encourage a U.S. agreement with Russia.

At the present time, NATO is moving into geopolitical and strategic overstretch, and U.S. unilateralism and Euro-provincialism must find, once again, common ground. A grand strategy would account for the following elements: Russia, the nature of threats and of future conflict, the price of NATO's enlargement, and the future of deterrence. At the present time, Europe does not have the United States of its wishes, nor does the United States have the Europe of its wishes—not a promising state for an alliance in the process of reinventing itself.

Successful Multilateralism

Unilateralism is the natural way for a hegemonic power to behave, but multilateralism was the secret of the United States' success for the second part of the twentieth century. The North Atlantic alliance has not fallen victim to its own success, but more than an ever more precarious, open-ended enlargement process is needed to give it coherence and a sense of direction. It will need a great deal of enlightened leadership on the part of the United States and the ability, present at the creation, to fuse the national U.S. interest with the interests of all the major and minor partners into a coherent whole. The Europeans, altogether or one by one, must widen their strategic horizon for Washington to consider seriously their concerns. ESDP must be devised strictly from within NATO; otherwise the bluff will be called. Even more important, Europeans must invest in Atlantic security to be a partner. If not, they will have a worse United States than they wish, but still a better United States than they deserve.

Pascal Boniface

The Specter of Unilateralism

$\mathbf{M}$any Americans, indeed many Westerners, believe that the French are anti-American by nature. No one in Washington would be surprised if a top-secret document, leaked from the Quai d'Orsay, revealed that French leaders spend their spare time thinking of ways to tweak the beak of the U.S. eagle. The myth of maverick France, personified by the larger-than-life figure of General Charles de Gaulle, is profoundly anchored in the collective imagination. Myths die hard. Nobody seems to notice that de Gaulle has been dead for more than 30 years and that the Franco–U.S. relationship has moved on.

Today, French opinion on how to approach the United States is far more nuanced. One can speak roughly of three main strands of French opinion. Some very influential French leaders and experts are aligned along two diametrically opposed, or polarized, attitudes, one supporting and one opposing the United States; between these, however, is the majority "moderate" attitude, which is what has made the Western alliance possible.

At one end of the polarized attitudes, some French support unfailing solidarity that at times even shades into docility. Those who possess this attitude argue that the United States should not be hindered in

Pascal Boniface is director of the Institute for International and Strategic Relations in Paris.

Copyright © 2001 by The Center for Strategic and International Studies and the Massachusetts Institute of Technology
The Washington Quarterly • 24:3 pp. 155–162.

discharging its global responsibility as the champion of democracy and security manager of the world. From this point of view, France should work toward supporting policies that benefit the Western community as a whole. National and personal interests must be set aside for the general interest. Some French strategic experts have built careers on being sharply critical of French policies that stray from the narrow paths defined by Washington, because a French expert who castigates the archaic ways of France will easily find a chorus of approval from across the Atlantic.

Opposing this polarized view is another, equally polarized viewpoint, in which everything the United States does is bad, or even malevolent, and every tragic event on the international scale is directly or indirectly a U.S. responsibility. These two extreme viewpoints are influential, but they are definitely in the minority. For most French—leaders, pundits, and ordinary citizens alike—France and the United States are ancient allies. The French have never forgotten the gratitude owed to the United States for its help in smashing the yoke of nazism and escaping the chains of communism. This majority viewpoint has sustained France as one of the most redoubtable allies of the United States during the defining crises of the Cold War, such as the Euro-missile crisis.

This attitude, however, does not translate into vassalage. Although France shares nearly all of the international objectives of the United States, the French definitely wish to preserve their right to differ on how these objectives should be achieved. Iraq epitomizes this desire of independence. The current difference in the attitudes of Paris and Washington should not belie the fact that both countries share the same final objective: to reintegrate Iraq into the community of nations as a democratic and peace-loving society. Ideally, realization of this goal would entail the removal of Saddam Hussein from power.

France participated energetically in the Persian Gulf War and in the sanctions regime against Iraq. Over the course of the last ten years, however, a rift has opened between the perceptions, not of Paris and Washington, but rather of Europeans on one side and the United States and Great Britain on the other. France, with Europe, believes that maintaining the current policy of embargoes and selective strikes has failed to weaken Hussein. Instead, the population has suffered, the country is devastated, and the dictator remains in power. From this perspective, the time to search for alternative solutions had come.

Washington, meanwhile, sees France as the chief culprit behind a premature move to end the sanctions regime and responds by accusing Paris of sacrificing the coalition's strategic interests for the sake of making a few francs. This jockeying between Paris and Washington is based more on a difference of tactics than of strategy and is more prominent in bilateral relations than it should be, thanks to the not-inconsiderable narcissism of both capitals, driven by an unshakeable belief in their mission to civilize the world.

The United States needs to be reassured that the French are keenly aware that an order of magnitude separates the realpolitik prospects of both countries. Only a U.S. president could claim, as Bill Clinton did, that the United States remains the world's only "indispensable nation." No doubt it is. Any belief that France could or would compete with the United States in terms of power would not only be illusory, but ridiculous. Competition as equals is out of the question.

Making a Virtue out of Necessity

Equality, in any case, is not what France seeks. Indeed, France coined the concept of the United States as a "hyperpower." When Minister of Foreign Affairs Hubert Védrine first used this neologism to qualify the new reality of U.S. power, he was sharply criticized both in France—where acknowledging U.S. supremacy is not politically correct—and in the United States—where the term "hyper" carries a negative connotation.

Védrine did not intend to pass judgment on U.S. power in his statement. He simply made an objective observation, reflecting a pragmatic attitude that acknowledges U.S. supremacy as a matter of course while trying to preserve some maneuvering room for France. France today is powerful enough to have worldwide interests, but not so powerful as to pursue its interests in an imperial fashion. Supporting this idea is the view that the collapse of the Soviet Union affords France the possibility to carve out a comfortable political niche: the role of the recalcitrant-but-indispensable ally that deals with the hard-to-handle sticky stuff that ultimately holds the Atlantic alliance together. Chance and necessity thus combine to produce equilibrium in France's foreign policy. Simply put, Paris makes a virtue out of necessity by insisting that Washington heed the opinions (or at least the existence) of other nations.

The dynamism of the U.S. economy during the 1990s has served as the driving force of world economic growth. The United States has indeed placed its power in the service of advancing and supporting democracy, toward a world of respect for all peoples and of collective security. The United States is indeed generally perceived as a champion of the universal values of peace, progress, and human dignity. The French, with other Europeans, share these same values and admire U.S. dynamism, diversity, ease of integration, and mobility.

This admiration is not universal. U.S. unipolarity and unilateral impulses are directly connected to the rift between the perceptions of Europeans and Americans. Europeans harbor deep doubts regarding certain aspects of U.S. society, such as the easy availability of firearms, the death penalty, the influence of money on the electoral process, social inequalities that are not only growing but accepted, the situation of African Americans, and the excessive commercialization of culture.

More to the point, on the international level, many Europeans deplore what the United States sometimes does with its supremacy. Perceptions prevail that the United States is increasingly tempted to pursue unilaterally defined policies with little regard for the interests and viewpoints of other nations, as if the United States confuses its national interest with a global interest. When once the saying was, "What is good for General Motors is good for the United States," now people in Washington are apparently saying, "What is good for the United States is good for the world." From this point of view, even if Washington's proclamations that U.S. power is beneficial to people everywhere are true, the self-glorification that seems customary to U.S. leaders (from "Manifest Destiny" to the "only indispensable nation") understandably does not cross the Atlantic well.

It's Unilateralism, Not Isolationism

The specter of U.S. isolationism, which haunted Western Europeans during the Cold War, has been replaced by the specter of U.S. unilateralism. Europeans are keenly sensitive to any sign that the United States intends to stray from the rules of multilaterally defined law, conceive a disaffection for international organizations, favor coercive practices, or in short, raise arguments that international rules place an unwarranted constraint on the freedom of the United States to act.

The United States would be wrong to think this sensitivity is uniquely French. It is, in fact, widely echoed elsewhere in Europe (even in Great Britain), whether by political leaders or the general population. In the long term, the most evident risk is that unilateralism will provide the fuel for anti-U.S. sentiment. This shift may already be happening among the younger generations, especially among university students (who nevertheless continue to attend U.S. universities).

Among the notable unilateral U.S. policies that particularly offend Europeans and the French are

- failing to sign the treaty banning antipersonnel mines;
- refusing to ratify the Comprehensive Test Ban Treaty;
- abrogating agreements on global warming regulations as defined in the Kyoto Protocol;
- bombing Iraq (with the British) and continuing the sanctions regime that chiefly harms the Iraqi general population, not Saddam Hussein;
- neglecting to acknowledge problems associated with North–South economic and developmental disparities;
- grudging willingness to assist in strengthening and legitimizing multilateral organizations, notably the United Nations (UN);
- tending to support Israel to the point where, in European public opinion, Israel appears more and more as the aggressor and the Palestinians as the victims; and
- seeking "defense" or "protection," which is defined in national terms, over "prevention," which is defined multilaterally.

Insofar as security policy is concerned, the United States and France view the problem of how to protect national territory from military threats quite differently. Generally speaking, from the French (and European) perspective, the main national security challenges presently come from collapsed states and zones of anarchy. In matters of security, the United States favors a coercive approach, including the U.S. tendency to confuse briefings for consultations.

Two Tests Ahead

Two strategic issues have revived the debate over the nature of the transatlantic alliance: the U.S. national missile defense (NMD) program and the effort to define a common European security and defense policy. By and large, the U.S. strategic rationale for NMD eludes Europeans. No one in Europe truly believes that North Korea is a military threat to the United States. No one doubts that the United States, which accounts for one-third of worldwide military expenditures, could deter a rogue nation. French and European leaders fear that the concept of NMD will revive the arms race, especially in Asia. Many believe this negative effect could precede the hypothetical deployment of NMD. When all is said and done, NMD, as the name suggests, is about a U.S. national plan; all protests to the contrary, the Europeans fully understand that they cannot prevent it. Washington should never forget—even once European governments stop publicly criticizing the NMD program or perhaps endorse it—that European public opinion generally rejects NMD. NMD will surely tarnish the U.S. image in Europe and the rest of the world.

With regard to the question of European defense, just as Franco–German reconciliation has been the driving force for Europe's economic reconstruction, it will provide the model for security structures. In the future, Paris and Berlin will be able to pursue a new model for cooperation, different from that of reconciliation between enemies: the successful "rebalancing" of the power relationship between friendly countries. France and Germany will accept such a rebalancing because it is premised on the existence of an overarching common objective.

During the East–West conflict, an asymmetrical parity existed between the power of France and Germany. The strategic autonomy of France provided a counterweight to the economic power of Germany. France's position as a permanent member of the UN Security Council and a nuclear-weapons state was complimented by the economic supremacy of Germany, which had a strong currency, trade surplus, and robust economy. Bluntly, France had the bomb while Germany had the mark.

Today, due to the drive for European unification, the French are a little Germanized, and the Germans are a little Frenchified. With the agony of division in the past, Germany has felt a new sense of maturity and exercises real sovereignty. France, too, is surer of itself than a decade ago, no longer approaching economic unification with Germany with the reflex of fear or mistrust. Symbolically and substantively, the euro has put an end to the franc/mark disparity and all its vexing technical and political issues. Americans should also come to terms with the need to rebalance their relationship with a Europe that can assume a larger strategic responsibility, now that it too is free from the burden of division.

In theory, the United States welcomes a European defense identity. In practice, however, the United States has a natural tendency to consider the relationship between the North Atlantic Treaty Organization (NATO) and European defense policy as a zero-sum game, fearing that any European move would detract from the cohesion of the alliance. The United States does not openly acknowledge that, to them, cohesion means "one, and only one, center of decision." Thus, quite a large gap exists between theory and practice. The closer we get to implementation of a Euro-defense, the stronger the misgivings of the United States. Just as de Gaulle was once famous for saying "non" to Washington, Washington has essentially defined three "non's" that, in its view, should shape this major step in European integration: nondecoupling of Europe from NATO, nonduplication of forces, and nondiscrimination against NATO countries that are not members of the European Union (EU).

A considerable contradiction thus arises. How can there be an egalitarian relationship if one party alone determines the nonnegotiable points of compatibility and incompatibility? Can the European Pillar of Defense have any meaning at all if its perimeter is strictly defined by Washington?

The Europeans need to convince the United States that the emergence of a European identity for defense and security is not contrary, and can even be helpful, to U.S. interests. By the same token, the United States can take into account the wishes of their European partners. Fortunately, this path has a precedent. Despite its military preeminence during the 1999 bombing of Yugoslavia, the United States accepted joint management of the conflict with the Europeans. This decision was not a military, but rather a political, necessity. Unilateral U.S. action in the region would have damaged the cohesion of the alliance and would not have allowed the United States the luxury it now enjoys of supplying only 20 percent of the Kosovo peacekeeping force.

The danger is that the United States will take the opposite view: that the emergence of an increasingly autonomous Europe means that the Western alliance will be rent by an ever-widening flaw. In this view, global disorder must be treated from a global perspective that only the United States can have; the EU, at best, can play only a secondary role to U.S. leadership. From this perspective, the most important thing is to strengthen the solidarity of the NATO alliance, as the plan for European defense autonomy entails an unacceptably high risk of decoupling or duplication of forces.

One could draw a parallel to the political dilemma that arrived with the French nuclear capability. At first vehemently opposed by the United States, one of the main arguments against French nuclear autonomy concerned the risk of duplication; after all, France's limited nuclear arsenal would provide only a marginal supplement to the overall nuclear capacity of the Atlantic alliance. Once the French *force de frappe* became a reality, however, the United States was obliged to accept it. Washington eventually made a virtue out of necessity—by acknowledging in the Ottawa Declaration of 1974 that France's nuclear capability was in fact useful for the defense of the West and for greater European security.

We should thus hope that the same recognition holds true for Europe today. The United States will no doubt do whatever it can to prevent actual defense autonomy from occurring, but that if Europe forges ahead, Washington will get used to it and will discover its value for the defense of the West.

As Kosovo exemplifies, unilateralism is certainly not the only way Americans can do business. On the contrary, the United States realized that it was better able to achieve its goal by playing the game of coalitions and compromise. In the long term, Europe's emergence in a well-balanced partnership with the United States can be in the U.S. interest, for the United States on its own will doubtfully be able to remain the world's security manager for long. After World War II, the leaders of France had the wisdom to reach out to the rising power of postwar Germany (with the delicate rebalancing act this action implied), no less for the sake of France than for the European values in which they believed. Similarly, today, the United States should have the wisdom to reach out to Europe, for its own good and for the sake of universal values.

Peter Ludlow

Wanted: A Global Partner

The description of the twentieth century as the American century was rarely if ever more appropriate than during the century's final decade. For seven bountiful years, the U.S. economy outperformed that of the European Union (EU) by a substantial margin. Even the productivity gap, which the continental European economies had done so much to narrow over the previous three decades, began to widen once again in the United States' favor. Militarily, the United States was even more obviously in a league of its own. To the bemusement of outside observers, the United States appeared determined to prepare for every imaginable contingency, not to mention some that, in European eyes at least, were scarcely imaginable. More mundanely, but still more significantly for those most immediately affected, the United States demonstrated in Bosnia, Dayton, and Kosovo that it can do things that even its most advanced allies cannot.

In this brave, new, unipolar world, rhetoric and reality easily intermingled. The United States ruled; the Anglo-Saxon model worked; Rhineland capitalism was doomed. Davos annually became the earthly tabernacle of a new cult whose high priests are English-speaking generators of wealth rather than the endearingly homespun prime ministers who come now to learn more than to guide. Guidance is something that,

Peter Ludlow is founding director of the Center for European Policy Studies.

Copyright © 2001 by The Center for Strategic and International Studies and the Massachusetts Institute of Technology
The Washington Quarterly • 24:3 pp. 163–171.

in the final analysis, only Alan Greenspan can claim to do. As for the EU, horror of horrors—its sluggish economy, its fumbling efforts to create a monetary union, its incurably rigid labor markets, its endless wrangling over arcane constitutional issues, its corrupt bureaucracy, its painfully slow expansion eastward, and its inability to police southeastern Europe have conspired to undermine the belief of all but the most faithful in a partnership of equals. Genuflection, it sometimes seems, has become the norm for Europeans, Japanese, and other erstwhile competitors wanting to make their way in Washington. Grovelling has become a profitable line of business for European journalists and broadcasters.

Although flattery may get the flatterer everywhere, it rarely gets the flattered anywhere. The economic lead that the United States enjoys over its nearest rivals is real enough. It is not, however, as big or as sustainable as it has often been made to appear. The rhetoric of success has in fact become a problem, inhibiting a balanced appreciation of the basis of the U.S. lead and thwarting any willingness to implement the changes in attitudes and practices that success itself entails.

Where Europe Stands

The U.S. gross domestic product (GDP) undoubtedly grew faster than the EU GDP in the mid- to late-1990s. In the long run, however, this trend will probably have little significance. The EU has grown faster during some periods and the United States has grown faster in others. The jury is still out on whether or not the new economy has created the basis for consistently higher growth rates in one jurisdiction or the other. Even if the foundation exists, nothing suggests that Europeans suffer from incurable defects permanently inhibiting them from tapping into its extra dynamism. On the contrary, evidence is growing that Europeans have already adjusted to the new economy further and faster than early estimates suggested. They start, after all, from a very high skill base. Productivity per employee per hour worked is now higher in France and some of the smaller EU economies than in the United States. Furthermore, notoriously low-productivity economies, such as

What Does the World Want from America?

the United Kingdom, have begun to show signs of catching up with their partners.

More importantly, the political revolution embodied in the European integration process has accelerated rather than slowed during the last ten years. The implementation of the Maastricht-based commitment to the Economic and Monetary Union has induced structural reforms of public finances and financial markets which might not have otherwise occurred as rapidly or effectively. Meanwhile, the single market program has continued to chip away at the vested interests and purblind mentality of protected national operators. Last, but by no means least, the European Council in March 2000 in Lisbon sanctioned a complex and extremely ambitious program of economic and social reform, reinforced by peer pressure and designed to eliminate obvious gaps between the EU and U.S. economies by 2010. The Lisbon conclusions contained a good deal of hyperbole, and some of the promises that the EU's heads of state or government made will almost certainly have to be redefined as the decade progresses. Doubts about detail should not, however, eclipse the overall significance of the event or the process that it initiated. The EU must develop even further before it becomes a single economy in the fullest sense. Thanks, however, to reforms started or completed during the years of the United States' latest phase of economic leadership, the EU, and more particularly the euro-zone, is less exposed to the fallout from a U.S. recession than it would otherwise have been.

At the same time, the EU has fostered fundamental changes in countries beyond its borders that in most cases had signaled their desire to join the EU immediately after the disappearance of their erstwhile Communist rulers. Citing the EU's management of eastward enlargement as yet another example of its inability to match the United States has become fashionable. Joining the North Atlantic Treaty Organization (NATO), however, is one thing; joining the EU quite another. NATO membership is a largely symbolic exercise, involving relatively painless changes in one significant, but nonetheless limited, segment of society. Entering the EU, by contrast, entails the total reorientation of legal codes, economic and social policies, and political as well as administrative systems toward European norms. Given the scale of the undertaking, entry before 2003 for the first group of candidates was never very likely.[1] The decision by the European Council in December 2000 in Nice to attempt incorporating the first entrants possibly in the first half of 2004 suggests that this highly ambitious undertaking is only slightly behind schedule. The increasing likelihood that the first group will include a majority of the 13 candidates puts this effort in a still more positive light.

The European Council virtually routinely reiterates the EU's determination to help Albania and the successor states of the former Yugoslavia to become members. At Nice, the council went further still, acknowledging Iceland, Norway, and Switzerland as prospective members.

The enlargement process is exceedingly complex and therefore difficult for outside observers to follow, much less get excited about it. Despite the progress that has been made, it will continue to run for years to come. Some of the prospective members may not enter for another 20–30 years. Others may fall by the wayside, either because their own domestic opinion will eventually veto entry, or because their governments will fail to deliver the economic, social, and political reforms on which the EU insists. In any transatlantic discussion of European security, however, it is impossible to ignore that, by moving toward a union of 35 members, the EU has begun to redraw the map of Europe, regardless of what the 2002 NATO summit may decide about NATO enlargement.

Even the hard security side of the story is not quite what it seems to be. Nobody can doubt U.S. military supremacy—least of all the Europeans—following events in Bosnia, Dayton, and Kosovo. The actual performance of the world's only superpower, however, has been distinctly patchy during the last 10 years, while Europe's contribution, both within and beyond its home continent, has been more impressive than commentators in Europe and the United States normally allow.

The U.S. decision to commit troops to Bosnia in 1995 was undoubtedly of decisive significance. So too was the contribution of its air forces in Kosovo. Yet, the principal driving force behind the EU's current and unexpectedly determined attempt to create a rapid reaction force has undoubtedly been anxiety about the continued dependability of the EU's transatlantic ally in the future, coupled with skepticism about whether an alliance that can seemingly only function in combat above 15,000 feet can be said to be truly operational.

The role played by the United States beyond Europe is also in question. U.S. military capability is quantitatively and qualitatively beyond the reach of any other power on earth. In light of what has actually happened in the last decade, what is the practical significance of this overwhelming military force? A decade after the U.S.-led coalition's victory in the Persian Gulf War, Saddam Hussein remains in power and U.S. policy toward Iraq appears increasingly implausible to most, if not all, the allies who joined the coalition in 1990. In the Middle East, the new administration may succeed where the Clinton presidency failed, but the current picture at any rate is one of a policy in ruins.

Meanwhile, the Europeans have managed to make a difference, even militarily. Perhaps not surprisingly, the EU member states provide the great majority of troops currently on the ground in the former Yugoslavia. More noteworthy, EU members are involved in 15 United Nations (UN) peacekeeping operations at a time when the United States is engaged in none outside southeastern Europe, where NATO operates under a UN mandate. Most striking of all, the EU is now irreversibly committed to creating a rapid reaction force of 60,000 persons and a civilian police force of 5,000 which can together or separately perform crisis management roles wherever the European Council decides to send them. There is still some way to go before this aspiration becomes operational. The EU's collective determination to move ahead, however, has already enabled a majority of member states to halt the seemingly inexorable decline of their defense budgets in the current year, prompted important organizational changes within Europe's political–military establishment, and built bridges between the EU's NATO members and their "neutral" partners.

Europeans should be the last group to resort to one-upmanship. The message is not therefore that Europe is better or stronger—which it quite clearly is not—but that claims such as those made by Secretary of State Colin Powell, at his confirmation hearing, that the United States has an interest "to lead, to guide, to help" in "every place on this earth" are simply not credible, whatever may have happened in the last seven years.[2] Nor are they relevant to the United States', let alone the world's, real needs.

The most important criticism of the extravagant rhetoric of the last few years is indeed not that it is unjustified by facts, but that it distracts those who indulge in it from a balanced appreciation of why the United States has flourished so conspicuously and what therefore are its own fundamental, long-term interests. As the major beneficiary to date of the new global economy, the United States should be more committed than any other player to sound global governance involving more rather than less multilateralism and to acknowledgement of the increasingly obvious fact that, in this interdependent world, international coalitions of nongovernmental actors have to be treated with a seriousness that governments have never before accorded them.

The United States that the European Union Needs

The United States that the EU needs is not a weak and sickly power. Nobody has gained from Japan's decline and fall. For the United States to follow a similar course would spell still more trouble, particularly for Europe. This situation is exactly the reverse of a zero-sum game. A strong United States is good for Europe, just as a strong EU is good for the United States. What is desired, therefore, is not a Lenten renunciation of wealth and power as much as a fundamental change of attitude toward the ways in which they are and should be deployed, grounded in a far reaching reappraisal of the nature of international politics at the beginning of the new millennium.

U.S. national security adviser Condoleezza Rice highlighted, from a European perspective, the true stakes in an article last year. U.S. foreign policy, she averred, should "proceed from the firm ground of the national interest, not from the interest of an illusory international community."[3] What is most disturbing in European eyes about Rice's statement is the assumption that a conflict between the pursuit of national interest and commitment to the interest of a far-from-illusory international community necessarily exists. The experience of the EU and its member states since the 1950s reveals the possibility of combining the robust defense of national interest with acquiescence in an international regime based on commonly agreed rules. Instead of destroying the nation-state, European integration has enhanced it by providing mechanisms through which every member, large and small, is better placed to safeguard its integrity. Individual member states have also acquired power and influence beyond its borders that they could not otherwise hope to have.

Lessons from European experience cannot, of course, be pushed too far. There are a lot of us, organized in a large number of states, occupying a territory much smaller than the United States. Europe is committed to "ever closer Union;" world government is by contrast a remote ideal. Analogies do exist, however, between the European microcosm and the global macrocosm in an era in which, thanks not least to the strength of the U.S. economy and the initiative of its entrepreneurs, globalization is a reality and no land on earth can escape its influence. The international community is not an illusion. Nor are the global challenges to the international economy, to the earth's ecological balance, and to the survival of free and democratic states figments of the imagination.

From this perspective, the pursuit of common interests and their encapsulation in common rules commonly administered are not luxuries, but necessities. Furthermore, these interests and rules are not incompatible with the exercise of leadership by the fit and the strong. On the contrary, France and Germany—to return for a moment to the European example—have exercised leadership in Europe more effectively through EU institutions than they could possibly have done outside them. The precondition of leadership within a multilateral regime founded on commonly formulated rules is, however, that the leader accepts the rules just as readily as the led. In addition, the effort to establish consensus with states that do not conform is only abandoned as a last resort and within the framework of the rules-based system.

Recasting the Transatlantic Dialogue

For the United States to become the kind of partner in global management that Europe and the rest of the world need, both the tone and the content of public debate and public policy must change. Composing a wish list of specific policy areas where a new approach is most urgently required would be relatively easy, if somewhat tedious, but a piecemeal discussion of this sort would only illustrate what is at stake. It would not tackle the underlying causes of the present malaise, which has its source in a collective failure to appreciate how much the global agenda has changed, and how the unbridled belief in the leadership of the world's only superpower—and the narrow definition of national interest which is its corollary—have ceased to be relevant or productive, in hard and soft security terms. The world neither needs nor wants an international order designed and maintained in Washington.

Obviously, such a radical shift in attitudes will not occur overnight. As Warren Buffett comes back into favor and Bill Gates seems slightly less superhuman, one can presumably expect some of the brasher tones of the last few years to disappear. The illusions that need to be banished are not, however, simply a consequence of economic success. On the contrary, they derive much of their strength from the fact that they correspond to deeply ingrained traditions and prejudices, which have themselves been reinforced by more recent cultural developments. The triumph of English as the language of the international community and the corresponding dominance of the Anglo-Saxon media in shaping world opinion are just two examples.

Given the depth and sophistication of the U.S. domestic debate about foreign policy, the primary catalysts of change will presumably be homegrown. Outside players can assume a role by challenging and exposing illusions, but no country can match the United States. As Samuel

Huntington has argued, however, a significant group of major regional powers exists which the United States ignores at its expense and which are capable of joint actions on their own account without prior consultation with Washington.[4]

First among these powers is the EU. To quote Huntington, "Healthy cooperation with Europe is the prime antidote for the loneliness of U.S. superpowerdom." If, however, the EU–U.S. relationship matures into the constructive partnership that it ought to be, it must undergo profound changes on both sides of the Atlantic.

As far as the United States is concerned, "changes" mean first and foremost accepting the EU as such as its most important partner in Europe. Given the structure of power in the EU, in which the European Council—the body that brings together the heads of state and government and the president of the commission—is the core of the EU executive, this realization does not mean that every dialogue must be routed via Brussels. On the contrary, as the Clinton administration demonstrated most effectively just prior to the European Council's decision in Helsinki to place Turkey on the same footing as other candidates for accession, successful lobbying entails applying pressure in member state capitals as well as on EU institutions. The decision to give Turkey equal status, like almost every other major strategic decision concerning Europe's future in recent decades, was nevertheless a collective decision of the European Council.

As this episode revealed, many in Washington know how to deal with the EU on important issues. The kind of systemic shift required, however, is more far-reaching. President Bill Clinton's frustration with the semi-annual EU–U.S. summits was understandable, given the banality of many if not most of the agendas during his administration. The fact that the meetings were so often low-key, however, was more a reflection of the value which even he placed on the partnership than, as his lieutenants frequently implied, the necessary consequence of too many meetings. If the leaders of the United States and the EU cannot find anything useful about which to talk, the notion of global governance has indeed a long way to go.

Two other illustrations of the much-needed paradigm change are worth mentioning. The first example involves the U.S. national security adviser yet again. Notably, neither she nor her coauthor, in an otherwise excellent monograph written six years ago on German unification,[5] showed any interest in the active participation of the European Commission in the negotiation of the State Treaty. The European perspective on the unification issue, developed through the European Council, effectively neutralized the damage that British prime minister Margaret Thatcher and French president François Mitterand might have done if left to their own devices. To ignore the European dimension of decisionmaking deprives the story of much of its meaning.

The other illustration concerns the development of a European military capability. The project is now so well advanced that it is difficult to imagine it being abandoned, although it is not yet changing the way in which those most deeply involved think about NATO. Words of approval for the plan are linked with warnings that the Europeans should not attempt to build a caucus within the alliance structures. If the process is not about building a caucus capable in certain circumstances of acting autonomously, however, it is difficult to understand what its purpose is. It is not, and it need not be, a threat to NATO, even though it will profoundly change NATO. Unless that realization is acknowledged, we are indeed headed for trouble.

If the United States needs to work with the EU, it needs an effective EU with which to work. Jean-Marie Soutou, former secretary general of the Quai d'Orsay, rightly observed that "Europe tends to get the U.S. partner that it deserves." If the EU wants the United States to take it seriously, it must itself be serious. The record of achievement during the last 50 years is remarkable. Europe has been transformed. An enormous amount is yet to be done.

If the EU looks to the United States to embrace multilateralism and global governance, it must itself assume a more significant global role, the details for which lie beyond the scope of this article. Although its role as the regional hegemonist obviously constitutes a large element of its claim to be treated as an important partner, the EU's credibility and therefore its powers of persuasion will suffer unless and until it makes a constructive and, where necessary, independent contribution to the development of the global system, in crisis management as much as trade and in creative diplomacy as well as aid. The lonely superpower needs global partners for it to heed the limits of superpowerdom and to appreciate the advantages of global governance. By raising its ambitions and reaching out on its own terms to other regional actors, the EU is arguably better placed than any other international player to facilitate the emergence of the United States that it and the world needs: a strong U.S. partner in a multilateral world order.

Notes

1. Peter Ludlow, *Preparing for Membership. The Eastward and Southern Enlargement of the EU* (Brussels: Centre for European Policy Studies, 1996), 74.

2. General Colin Powell, testimony before the U.S. Senate Foreign Relations Committee, January 17, 2001.

3. Condoleezza Rice, "Promoting National Interest," *Foreign Affairs* 79, no. 1 (January/February 2000).

4. Samuel Huntington, "The Lonely Superpower," *Foreign Affairs* 78, no. 2 (March/April 1999).

5. Condoleezza Rice and Philip Zelikow, *Germany United: Europe Transformed* (Cambridge: Harvard University Press, 1995).

Maria Claudia Drummond

Guide Globalization into a Just World Order

President John F. Kennedy's inspired words in 1963 could well be seen as prophetic today: "What kind of peace do we seek? Not a *Pax Americana* enforced on the world by American weapons of war ... not merely peace for Americans but peace for all men and women—not merely peace in our time but peace in all time." Envisaging a world illuminated by a universal peace based on consent and awareness and not on military power, Kennedy expressed the humanistic ideals that should be guiding the foreign policy formulation of the world's most powerful nation in the age of globalization.

As the values inherent to the democratic system of government become internationally accepted as those principles that best can assure humankind's well-being, global legitimating regulations become crucial. Two kinds of systems are discernible in today's world: regional integration arrangements, characterized by various levels of complexity and regulation; and the global system of the United Nations (UN), with its specialized agencies and financial institutions.

With these standards come more questions. What are the changes transforming the world at a vertiginous pace, resulting in the parallel

Maria Claudia Drummond is the Federal Senate of Brazil's legislative adviser for foreign relations and Mercosul and technical adviser to the Joint Parliamentary Committee of Mercosul.

Copyright © 2001 by The Center for Strategic and International Studies and the Massachusetts Institute of Technology
The Washington Quarterly • 24:3 pp. 173–183.

movements of globalization and regionalism? What is the role of the United States in Latin America, and what are the prospects for cooperation? What is the role of the United States in reformulating the global system?

A Changed World

The predicted obsolescence of the nation-state as the primary political unit—entitled to absolute sovereignty, to be the dominant actor in international relations, and to be the only subject of international law—is not a new concern for experts in international relations. The increasing influence of multinational corporations in the 1970s resulted in the emergence of the "market," instead of the nation-state, as the key political actor.

In fact, the nation-state lacks appropriate tools and mechanisms to deal with those issues typical of an interdependent world. The internationalization of the economy and of production, expressed in the increased prominence of multinational corporations and the instant flow of investment across the globe made possible by computer and satellite, have superceded the old nation-state, in a way.

Issues such as terrorism, drug trafficking, environmental preservation, the rational use of natural resources, and the spread of contagious diseases have acquired an international dimension. One nation's sulfurous smoke becomes another nation's acid rain. No single nation-state, powerful as it may be, can deal effectively, by itself, with such issues. The threats to security that the nation-state must address are no longer necessarily of a military nature. They require conscious regulation, either on the regional or global level or on both, which can only result from mechanisms of cooperation devised by the nation-states themselves. As Hobbes wrote, what makes men give up their independence is fear.[1]

Additionally, the increased importance of economic issues has blurred the line between those themes that belong to the international sphere and those that are purely domestic. The impact of the flow of international investment on domestic economies is an obvious example. Global finance can generate crises that are capable of destroying emerging economies that are not based on sufficiently sound macroeconomic foundations.

The processes of economic integration simultaneously underway in different parts of the world represent another feature of the globalized world. Different mechanisms, ranging from free-trade areas to monetary unions, are being utilized and are making progress on all five continents.[2] These processes, needless to say, impact the productivity of the state. Mercosul (the Common Market of the South), for example, has had to cope with a number of conflicts involving some of its most productive sectors, such as textiles, poultry, dairy, and shoe production. As a result, ordinary citizens are not surprisingly becoming more interested in their government's foreign trade and policy decisions.

In addition, events such as the Persian Gulf War, the cruelty of ethnic cleansing in the Balkans, brutal violence in Somalia, and genocide in Rwanda make the contemporary world painfully aware of its own shortcomings and limitations. In other words, the celebrated new world order that many scholars thought would emerge, bringing peace and prosperity for all, is proving to be more like chaos and anarchy.

Thus "the spaceship called Earth" desperately needs a captain and a vision of the route. In this grim scenario, what role should the United States ideally play vis-à-vis its neighbors and, ultimately, the world?

From Intervention to Cooperation in Latin America?

Latin Americans have sound reasons to be suspicious and hesitant when the United States proposes initiatives such as building a free-trade area comprising the entire hemisphere. In fact, Latin American countries have experienced the effect of U.S. interventionism far too many times.

Under the Monroe Doctrine of 1823, the United States declared that it would refrain from interfering in Latin America and that the imperial powers of Europe should also respect the independence of their former colonies. The declaration was aimed at the Caribbean, because the Europeans were still active in that region, and was intended to identify the vital interest of the United States in an area it considered to be its own inland sea.

Only much later, in 1898, was a policy of intervention first used. Based on the principles enunciated in the Monroe Doctrine, the United States went to war to expel the Spanish from Cuba and Puerto Rico. At that time, the United States believed that it had an obligation to bring freedom and democracy to its smaller brothers in Latin America. The result was quite different. Puerto Rico became a U.S. colony, and Cuba's freedom was curtailed by the Platt amendment, under which the United States reserved for itself the right to intervene in Cuban affairs "for the preservation of Cuban independence and the maintenance of a government adequate for the protection of life, property, and individual liberty."[3]

By 1898, substantial U.S. investment was flowing into Cuba. In 1904, President Theodore Roosevelt stated his corollary to the 1823 Monroe Doctrine in a speech to Congress, turning the United States into a sort of policeman that could "exercise an international police power" in flagrant cases of "wrong-doing" on the American continent. During this period, Panama was seized from Colombia to create a canal zone under U.S. sovereignty; and U.S. troops occupied Nicaragua from 1912 to 1933, Haiti from 1915 to 1934, and the Dominican Republic from 1916 to 1924.

U.S. "gunboat diplomacy" on the continent resulted in accusations of imperialism and interventionism. A pan-American council was established under the "Good Neighbor Policy" of President Franklin D. Roosevelt, who shifted from unilateral action by the United States to collective action by all the American republics. The charter of the Organization of American States (OAS), signed in Bogotá, Colombia, in 1948 seemed to set up a more democratic and balanced framework for relations among the American republics, stating in Article 15 that "no state or group of states has the right to intervene, directly or indirectly, for any reason whatever, in the internal or external affairs of any other state."

In spite of the formidable repudiation of intervention contained in the OAS charter, and given the fact that the United States was preoccupied during the Cold War with the Soviet Union, the question became whether the United States would refrain from intervention if a Communist government came into power in a Latin American republic.

The answer would come only six years later. In 1954, the freely elected government of Guatemala nationalized the U.S.-owned electrical company and told the United Fruit Company that it would have to release 200,000 acres of land. The OAS approved a declaration stating that "the domination or control of the political institutions of any American state by the international [C]ommunist movement" would constitute a threat to the sovereignty and political independence of the American states. Although the major democracies of Latin America had voted against it, the declaration allowed the Central Intelligence Agency to overthrow the government of Guatemala; subsequent governments returned Guatemala to dictatorial rule, supported by its right-wing oligarchies.

The turning point in U.S.–Latin American relations was Fidel Castro's decision to defy Washington and move Cuba into the Communist camp, an action preceded by vociferous protests against the United States on the occasion of President Richard Nixon's visit to Caracas in 1958. No wonder the State Department was shaken by these events in the most crucial Cold War years: Latin America's presence in the Western sphere of influence had been taken for granted by Washington since the end of World War II.

The United States used direct military intervention again at Santo Domingo in the spring of 1965, arousing apprehension in Latin America. This trend continued with U.S. military intervention in Latin America in Grenada (1983), Panama (1989), and Haiti (1994) to accomplish U.S. foreign policy objectives. In Panama, "Operation Just Cause" pledged to safeguard U.S. lives, defend democracy, combat drug traffic, and protect the integrity of the Panama Canal Treaty. In Haiti, "Operation Restore Democracy" returned Haiti's elected president, Jean-Bertrand Aristide, to power.[4]

For the United States, any attempt by Latin American countries to change their archaic structures and address a feudal land-owning aristocracy that refused to relinquish any of its privileges seemed to bring the danger of a pro-Communist regime seizing control of the government. The principle of nonintervention, however, is ingrained in Latin American culture. It involves the very question of national independence—a cause that Latin Americans cherish—which enjoys a rare unanimity among the common people, governing elites, and intellectuals and which maintains an importance that the anti-Communist crusade has never overshadowed. Because of this principle, Latin Americans never supported Kennedy's Alliance for Progress, which was devised as an instrument of social reform: the elites rejected it, fearing loss of privileges, and the intellectuals were suspicious of it.

During that period, studies by the Economic Commission for Latin America emerged, recommending economic integration as an effective instrument for the industrialization of Latin America. The first Montevideo Treaty was signed in 1960, creating the Latin American Free Trade Association (LAFTA). Andean and Caribbean countries adopted subregional integration mechanisms without much success.

The atmosphere of social unrest and political instability on the continent would soon give way to the establishment of a number of military, right-wing dictatorships throughout Latin America. The integrationist movement did not seem to rally much support either from the United States or from the deeply nationalistic military governments.

The 1970s brought the oil and debt crises. By joining the Organization of Petroleum Exporting Countries (OPEC), some Latin American countries made a gesture of independence from Western influence and, furthermore, defied the 1975 U.S. trade bill that excluded from its benefits nations that joined cartels to raise raw materials prices.

During the 1980s, Latin American countries began two initiatives that seemed to assert their will to pursue policies independent from U.S. participation. First, economic integration was revived with the celebration of a second Montevideo Treaty, which replaced LAFTA with a more flexible integration mechanism called the Latin American Integration Association (LAIA). Second, a forum for political consultation was established, called the Rio Group, comprising only Latin American countries, aimed at first as a means to pacify the military conflict in

Central America, and later as a forum to discuss issues of primary concern for Latin America, such as foreign debt.

By the middle of the decade—as most Latin American countries under military regimes gradually returned to democracy—a new initiative toward integration took shape. Initially, it involved only the two largest economies in the Southern Cone, Argentina and Brazil. In 1991, with Uruguay and Paraguay joining, the Asunción Treaty was signed, thus creating Mercosul, the first economic bloc in Latin America whose impact on the flow of regional trade was capable of attracting the attention of both the United States and the European Union. Trade among the Mercosul countries increased more than 400 percent in eight years, reaching about $20 billion in 1998.

By the time the Asunción Treaty was signed, countries like Brazil, Argentina, and Mexico had industrialized further, and their exports had ceased to depend as heavily as before on raw materials and commodities. Most Latin American countries were now under democratic regimes and were making a tremendous effort to implement the necessary reforms—both economic and institutional—that would allow their economies to better participate in the globalized world. A report issued by CSIS in December 1999, regarding the transformations sweeping Latin America in the 1990s, stated, "The new attitude of public- and private-sector leaders represents a philosophical sea change regarding the role of government, the importance of more liberalized markets, the salience of more transparent institutions, and the impact of technology."[5]

A New Regional Relationship

With the end of the Cold War, and relative political and economic stability in Latin American countries, a new era has begun in the relationship between the United States and Latin America, now focused on trade and investment rather than on security and ideology.

In the early 1990s, President George Bush made the first proposals related to the Initiative for the Americas Enterprise. Just three months after the establishment of Mercosul, in June 1991, the four Mercosul countries and the United States signed an agreement establishing a Consultative Council on Trade and Investment to "pursue a growing opening of markets between the United States and the four South American countries."

Having successfully concluded the North American Free Trade Agreement with Mexico and Canada, the Clinton administration sponsored a 1994 summit in Miami for all democratically elected heads of state in the region to launch an ambitious project aimed at establishing a Free Trade Area of the Americas (FTAA). The Declaration of Principles signed on that occasion pledged the determination of the 34 countries to "establish a partnership for development and prosperity based on democracy, free trade, and sustainable development." It further recognized "the heterogeneity and diversity of the resources and cultures on the continent." The proposal met with a mixed reaction in Latin America. Although some sectors perceive the potential advantages it entails, suspicion exists that the FTAA might have been devised to benefit only U.S. interests, particularly in light of the size of the U.S. economy compared to the rest of the hemisphere (the United States accounts for 70 percent of the hemisphere's gross national product).

Latin America's heavy reliance on exports of commodities and agricultural products, a highly protected sector in industrialized countries, is widely known. During the last decade, Washington raised the subsidies given to U.S. agricultural producers by 300 percent, or $32 billion, annually. Of course, these policies do not bolster the confidence of Latin American countries in the fairness of the negotiations leading to an FTAA. How can the United States preach the virtues of free trade and open markets while adopting domestic policies that distort competition in the international market? If the United States is prepared to address the sensitive issues that interest Latin American countries, such as agriculture and antidumping actions, and if negotiations are based on reciprocity—decisionmaking by consensus, single undertaking (i.e., nothing is agreed until everything is agreed), and market access in all sectors—then the relationship between the United States and Latin America will surely have reached a new cooperative level.[6]

This new level of cooperation requires U.S. respect for standing agreements within the framework of other integration initiatives under way in Latin America, such as Mercosul. Latin American countries have had to come a long way to perceive themselves finally as belonging to the same region, sharing a common heritage in terms of history, language, and creed. Latin Americans cherish this achievement of a new level of understanding.

Latin Americans may be somewhat suspicious of a certain ideological bias that, in spite of the end of the Cold War, may persist in the U.S. approach to the complex realities of the region. This kind of approach may result in a failure to grasp some of the region's more subtle aspects, those that escape old labels. One undesirable consequence of this failure would be the opening of a communication gap between U.S. negotiators and their Latin American counterparts.

Respect for the rich cultural diversity present in 34 nations is essential. Although the United States must be proud of its culture of capitalism and democracy, the decade-old experience of Mercosul shows the importance of approaching negotiations, no matter how asymmetrical the partners, in a spirit of consultation and equality. Unity is not possible if diversity is not recognized and respected.

The absence of Cuba from the FTAA is another aspect of the initiative that deserves further thought. The guiding values and conditions enshrined in the 1994 declaration—democratic rule, respect for human rights, and free elections—would, by themselves, exclude the possibility of Cuban participation in the initiative. Yet Mexico, Venezuela, and Brazil maintain friendly relations with Cuba and are opposed to the trade embargo imposed by the United States. The question is, what if Cuba complies with the requirements set out in the declaration and holds free elections? If a pro-Socialist government is elected, and if Cuba requests to join the FTAA, would the United States support Cuba's candidacy, in defiance of the fierce opposition of the Cuban American community in Florida? This issue is potentially explosive and would certainly provoke friction within the region.

The U.S.-funded, $1.3 billion military component in Plan Colombia to eradicate the coca trade—opposed by Venezuela, Brazil, Cuba, and Mexico—is another point that might slow FTAA negotiation. The U.S. military presence in Latin America will always be perceived as a new version of the interventionist policy of Cold War times.

Shaping a Changed World

Along with regionalism, a global system is operating that escapes any and all attempt at regulation. The Commission on Global Governance, an independent group of 28 leaders,[7] was established in 1992 with UN support to suggest ways in which our global community could better manage its affairs. In its 1995 report, the Commission wrote, "Our common future will depend on the extent to which people and leaders around the world develop the vision of a better world and the strategies, the institutions, and the will to achieve it."[8]

These conclusions represent a powerful and urgent call to the world's governments. Changes are taking place at a breathtaking pace and on a global scale. One of the most crucial effects of the globalization process is the widening gap between rich and poor. As the Commission's report emphasized, "A sophisticated, globalized, and increasingly affluent world currently coexists with a marginalized global underclass, and this in itself represents a threat both on the national level, but also to the stability of the international system." As a result, "[g]lobal security must be broadened from its traditional focus on the security of states to include the security of people and the planet." Not one international organization currently offers the tools required to deal with the multifaceted aspects of change.

Although specialized agencies—such as the United Nations Educational, Scientific and Cultural Organization, the World Food and Agriculture Organization, and the World Health Organization—enjoy widespread recognition for the priceless services they have rendered humanity, 50 years after San Francisco, the UN is viewed as a feeble body, inefficient and dispensable, in the eyes of many.

On the other hand, the World Trade Organization (WTO), a more recent creation that emerged from the Uruguay Round of the General Agreement on Tariffs and Trade, presents a dynamic feature of governance: it includes a dispute settlement mechanism. The WTO covers only a limited range of issues, however, and is restricted to trade and investment in areas such as goods, services, intellectual property, anti-dumping, subsidies, and government procurement.

During his first inaugural address in 1993, President Bill Clinton said:

> Profound and powerful forces are shaking and remaking the world, and the urgent question of our time is whether we can make change our friend and not our enemy. ... There is no longer division between what is foreign and what is domestic—the world economy, the world environment, the world AIDS crisis, the world arms race—they affect us all. ... Today, as an old order passes, the new world is more free but less stable. Communism's collapse has called forth old animosities and new dangers. Clearly America must continue to lead the world we did so much to make.

This new world calls for the new values of global humanism. Life, liberty, and the pursuit of happiness are not unfamiliar to Americans; they inspired the Founding Fathers. Now these values should be pursued on a global scale. In the new world, seeing millions living near absolute poverty levels and lacking access to safe water and sanitation is no longer tolerable. The development of telecommunications has progressed to allow shocking images of misery to invade our homes and our consciences. Outrageous inequalities coexist with unprecedented levels of prosperity, both within and among countries. The new world order must meet global needs, rather than serve a state-centered version of vested interests. Global humanism presupposes fundamental shifts in the planetary distribution of wealth, environmental protection, and rules of trade and investment that should contemplate the asymmetries between the industrialized and the emerging and low-income economies.

Some have called our time the "age of the environment," others the "age of globalization," the "information era," or the "e-age." President Fernando Henrique Cardoso once called it "an age of citizenship."[9] Indeed, the public protests that have been taking place wherever multilateral economic meetings are held do not leave any doubt about the existence of an emerging transnational society. Its organized groups are clamoring for participation in the international decisionmaking process.[10]

The challenge then is to devise instruments for the promotion of democratic, global citizenship. Cardoso wrote, "To avoid facile solutions, we must squarely confront the fact that there is a deficit of democratic citizenship at the international level and insist that progressive governance expand beyond the domestic scene." This path involves, of course, mechanisms and institutions that should allow democratic accountability and transparency in the international decisionmaking processes. Globalization has created unparalleled concentrations of autocratic power that must be brought under democratic control; otherwise, they will produce poverty and despair for countless millions.[11]

The United States is the home of the oldest democracy in the world. It is the world's leading power and its most prosperous economy. Its leadership is unchallenged. It has a vibrant civil society. The United States is thus the natural leader to help everyone devise and support the strategies and institutions needed to promote governance of the global society. Among these strategies, UN reform and enhancement would be at the forefront, principally by providing for a more democratic decisionmaking system that would phase out the veto and allow for representatives of a global civil society. Restructuring the architecture of the Bretton Woods institutions; mobilizing international support for implementing Agenda 21, as agreed at the 1992 Rio De Janeiro Conference on Environment and Development; adopting trade and investment regulations that take into account the asymmetries between emerging and low-income economies and the industrialized countries; and strengthening international law by supporting the work of the World Court and the establishment of the International Criminal Court, the statute of which was approved in Rome in July 1998, are other urgent initiatives.[12]

Global governance depends on leadership. After World War II, the United States led the planning process that produced the UN system. Now, as the world faces transformations that once more threaten its survival, the United States must exercise its leadership to create a renewed system of global governance. This action requires political courage, sustained by an ethical vision that goes beyond city, state, and country to encompass the whole of humanity. By doing so, the United States would be acknowledging each country's responsibility for the well-being of the planet. Surely this endeavor will not be an easy task, and it will face opposition at home and abroad. As Václav Havel said, however, when addressing the U.S. Congress in 1990:

> We are still incapable of understanding that the only genuine backbone of all our actions—if they are to be moral—is responsibility: responsibility to something higher than my family, my country, my firm, my success, responsibility to the order of being where all our actions are indelibly recorded and where, and only where, they will be properly judged.

Perhaps expecting the United States to play that role is wishful thinking. No other country, however, in this crucial time in human history, is more capable of creating a safer and more equitable era for itself and for its global neighborhood than the United States.

Notes

1. Adam Watson, *The Evolution of International Society* (London: Routledge, 1992).

2. Examples of these processes are the European Union, the Andean Community, the Caribbean Common Market, Mercosul, NAFTA, ASEAN, GCC (Gulf Cooperation Council), and so forth.

3. See Watson, *Evolution of International Society*, 198.

4. See Charles W. Kegley Jr. and Eugene R. Wittkopf, *American Foreign Policy* (New York: St. Martin's Press, 1996).

5. See Georges Fauriol and William Perry, *Thinking Strategically about 2005: The United States and South America*, CSIS Americas Program Report, December 1999.

6. Rubens Barbosa, "A View from Brazil," *Washington Quarterly* 24, no. 2 (Spring 2000).

7. Among the officials on the commission were Ingvar Carlsson (Sweden), Shridaath Rampal (Guyana), Oscar Arias (Costa Rica), Barber Conable

(United States), Jacques Delors (France), Enrique Iglesias (Uruguay), Celina do Amaral Peixoto (Brazil), and Maurice Strong (Canada).

8. Commission on Global Governance, *Our Global Neighbourhood* (Oxford: Oxford University Press, 1995).

9. Fernando Henrique Cardoso, "An Age of Citizenship," *Foreign Policy* (Summer 2000).

10. Recent examples include Seattle during the WTO Ministerial Meeting in November 1999, that failed to launch the Millennium Round; and in April 2000 in Washington and in October of that same year in Prague, during meetings of the International Monetary Fund and the World Bank.

11. International Baha'i Community, "Who Is Writing the Future?" (New York, 1999).

12. See Commission for Global Governance, *Our Global Neighbourhood*.

Part II: How the Reflection Looks to the United States

Simon Serfaty

The New Normalcy

The future has far too much imagination. To face it, fragments of the past are used as flashlights for the unpredictable events that loom ahead. Once in a while, however, the batteries run out and the observer is left in the dark. A decade ago, the fall of the Soviet empire was said to be one such moment. That claim was exaggerated. Throughout the Cold War, the Soviet collapse had often been envisioned as part of the future. Sadly, believing it unthinkable said more about us than about our then-adversary.

When friends abroad were invited to outline their preferences of the U.S. role in the world for the coming years in *The Washington Quarterly*'s "Through the Looking Glass" section last summer, they provided a surprisingly coherent vision—a vision that conveyed more about their respective national or regional perspectives than about the United States and its own aspirations. That all found the United States to be at least "first among equals" was hardly surprising. Yet, some praised its "unconditional viability" as a "virtual buffer state" in areas of regional conflicts, while others complained of the "unbearable lightness" of a leadership that places "too

Simon Serfaty is a professor of U.S. foreign policy with the graduate program in international studies at Old Dominion University in Norfolk, Virginia. He also serves as director of the Europe Program at CSIS and is the author of numerous books, including the recent *Memories of Europe's Future: Farewell to Yesteryear*.

Copyright © 2002 by The Center for Strategic and International Studies and the Massachusetts Institute of Technology
The Washington Quarterly • 25:2 pp. 209–219.

much emphasis on threat perception" and expects too many "quick results that will not be delivered." With most foreign observers, if not all, in agreement that "competition as equals is out of the question," a competition seemed to ensue for privileged status. Thus, regional viceroys or even "global partners" were identified to balance a dangerous unilateralist temptation—a tendency "to confuse briefings for consultation."[1]

Most foreign observers of U.S. policies in the world, critics and well-wishers alike, understood clearly that, at their best, U.S. policies are "honest" (meaning the United States is an "honest broker") but not disinterested. Call it "unconditional primacy" and pray for it to be prudent, attentive, watchful, flexible, sensitive, and more. Otherwise, rejoice that if "what is right is in U.S. interests," what is good for the United States will be right for the world (or at least, according to Barry Rubin, for the Middle East)—even if occasionally "less is more" (or at least, added Dmitri Trenin, for Russia). In either case, there could be no escape from, or for, the last great power left standing at the end of the twentieth century and thus bound to lead at the start of the twenty-first century. In the absence of any credible counterweight among those who view such sustained U.S. leadership "with either ambivalence or outright disdain," the few available counterparts could only aspire to small, supportive roles. Thus, "interpreters of the Asian mind" and "special allies" in Europe that "appreciate U.S. purposes and power" could be "forces for stability in world politics."

When "Through the Looking Glass" was written, the events of September 11 had not yet occurred—nor could they be anticipated, as they were truly unprecedented. Now, the future seems to have been fundamentally altered, but the nature of these alterations is not yet clear. A year after the departure of President Bill Clinton, a new normalcy belies the best that was expected of the past decade and the worst that was anticipated for the new one.

False Starts and New Beginnings

Even under conditions of constitutional normalcy, which were lacking in November 2000, presidential transitions are moments of enthralling chaos and flawed certainties, as the nation's agenda forces a new president away from his campaign rhetoric and even, on occasion, his personal convictions. Especially in the context of foreign and security policy, patterns of change and continuity ignore the electoral calendar, and predictions made during such transitions are, therefore, often misleading. Indeed, despite a combative rhetoric of dissent, continuity from one president to the next is usually the norm; significant changes are most likely to occur within each presidential administration.

In other words, every president becomes what he did not want to be. Since 1945, the pattern has periodically repeated. President Harry Truman initially had limited postwar foreign policy goals—mainly Europe and maybe Japan—but the Korean War set the stage for the globalist exuberance of the 1950s. President John F. Kennedy was a charismatic cold warrior, until he discovered the need for détente after the 1962 Cuban missile crisis—too late, however, to get the nation out of the interventionist trap that buried Lyndon B. Johnson. After the 1972 Moscow summit, President Richard Nixon returned to the joys of containment in the Middle East and central West Africa; and his successor, President Gerald Ford, ultimately banned references to "détente" for the duration of the 1976 presidential campaign. President Jimmy Carter viewed the Nixon–Henry Kissinger–Ford foreign policy as the antimodel of what he wanted to do, but relentless Soviet pressures in Iran, Afghanistan, and even Central America forced a reappraisal of his penchant for human rights. More recently, President Ronald Reagan, the staunch warmonger who dismissed the idea of negotiations with the "evil empire," left office as a peacemaker. Clinton, who had wanted to come home in order to attend to "the economy, stupid," made the world his new home after his unpresidential behavior took him away from his original emphasis on domestic themes and issues.

In January 2001, the Clinton legacy that conditioned the new president's goals and aspirations was poor. Unusually popular abroad, Clinton was an acrobat who dared to start everything but failed to complete anything—in the greater Middle East, Southeastern Europe, Northern Ireland, the Aegean, and in the Korean Peninsula. With regard to defeated countries (Russia and Iraq), ascending powers (China and Europe), and failed states (North Korea and Afghanistan), Clinton's goals proved all the more elusive because the will was lacking, the commitment remained ambivalent, the interests were ill-defined, and the attention was short-lived. Similarly, with regard to security institutions (NATO enlargement), as well as global organizations (such as the World Trade Organization and the United Nations (UN)) and their new agenda (such as health issues and the environment), the rhetoric remained ahead of the commitment, the commitment short of capabilities, the capabilities separate from interests, and the interests beyond public comprehension.[2]

Thus, the Clinton legacy of unfinished business forced on President George W. Bush an urgency that complicated further the late start caused by the unsettled November elections. The errors the president and his advisers made in the spring were neither sins of arrogance nor expressions of bellicosity. Rather, it was as if the more senior members of the new team had forgotten the experience gained during their previous years of service. In some ways, the new foreign and security team was like the Carter team that, back in 1977, had also come to office with an exaggerated sense of what could be accomplished and how quickly. "Every action we've taken," explained Zbigniew Brzezinski at the time, "was part of a plan for the first 90 days ... [that] was carried out systematically."[3] In 2001 the new president might not have had any such game plan, if only because of a transition spent waiting for the election to end. His determination to rely on Clinton as an antimodel, however, and his senior national security advisers' recommendation to act swiftly, had sharpened during the eight previous years.

The Bush administration did not live long, however, with its campaign rhetoric. Thoughts of an impending withdrawal of U.S. troops in Kosovo soon disappeared. The "national" dimension of missile defense was pointedly removed; consultations with allies, friends, and potential foes were eagerly sought. The new president's alleged intention to confront Russia with U.S. missile defenses, strategic deep cuts, and NATO expansion gave way to his emotional forays into Russian president

Vladimir Putin's soul. Notwithstanding a looming "nuclear" battle over foreign sales corporations and other perennials of transatlantic economic relations, the Bush administration embraced Europe's interest in a millennium round of trade negotiations—a step Clinton had resisted.

Nor was this evolution limited to the facts or perceptions of the administration's policies and attitudes toward Europe. Thus, the muscles flexed throughout the presidential campaign as a direct warning to Iraqi president Saddam Hussein were relaxed, and U.S. secretary of state Colin Powell urged the UN to enforce sanctions that would be more effective but also more compassionate. The decision to end negotiations with North Korea was reconsidered in early June. After the potentially catastrophic clash with China in the spring, the president's voice lost its earlier harshness, and Bush *fils* began to speak with the same soothing tones his father used a decade earlier. Meanwhile, threats to allow monetary crises to run their course rather than risk the "moral hazards" of bailing out states in financial difficulties were ignored to help Turkey and cry for Argentina.

In short, by the end of the summer of 2001, the Bush administration was responding to earlier patterns of presidential transitions—patterns of false starts and new beginnings. The new beginning that could be observed as the new president learned more about allies and adversaries, as well as ascending powers and failed states, however, was to prove to be another false start. The attacks against the World Trade Center and the Pentagon awakened the United States to international anarchy that had been mainly ignored during the previous decade but now threatened to define a new normalcy for the United States and the rest of the world.

The New Normalcy

Absent a debate over the durability of U.S. preponderance, the sustainability of U.S. leadership as a matter of will (that of the nation) and also as a matter of competence (including that of the president) may have been at issue after Clinton left office. That situation existed, however, before the events of September 11 seemed to reinforce the centrality of U.S. power, as well as the desirability of the leadership required to manage it effectively. "The way I think of it, it's a new normalcy," said U.S. vice president Richard Cheney in late October. With the war itself such "that it may never end, [at] least, not in our lifetime," Cheney warned that the post–September 11 conditions "will become permanent features in our ... way of life."[4]

Admittedly, the new normalcy is in part a narcissistic reflection on the privileged history of the nation—a history of physical invulnerability and cultural uniqueness. Others often asked the United States, as it waged wars abroad, to understand the history of those countries on whose behalf it was fighting. Now, this need has been reversed: other countries should understand the history of the country leading them to battle. The loss of territorial virginity caused by the terrorist rape of U.S. cities will dominate the nation's collective memory for generations to come. This event is not just about human lives, however tragic their losses were. It is about history forcing itself on a U.S. experience that was designed to defeat the evils of history. For the United States to lose the battle against terror would be to abandon the country to fears that were supposedly confined to others. Telling U.S. citizens that this situation is the way of history will not do. That is not the American way.

The logic of the new U.S. thinking would be enough to sustain U.S. leadership, but it might not be enough to sustain the support of other countries. The events of September 11 also unveiled the risks of a new anarchy that finds Thomas Hobbes' First Man, with a life that is "poor, nasty, brutish, and short," rebel against a pampered Last Man who, in the words of Putin, "had grown fat, slow, and lost [his] capacity for resistance."[5] The new normalcy Cheney and the followers of U.S. leadership fear is, therefore, neither war nor terror but an unusual mixture that resembles no past threat of organized violence. As deterrence of the groups willing (let alone able) to inflict such violence ceases to be credible, preemption becomes the only reliable solution. As protection of one is unlikely to be effective without contributions from many, coalitions are required to attend to the various dimensions of collective security in ways that are complementary even if they cannot be common. In other words, the new normalcy has put to rest whatever urge for retrenchment the new U.S. administration might have felt in early 2001. The "over there" of yesteryear's wars, as recent as Kosovo, has become the "over here" of today's conflicts, lest the fear of terror becomes a way of life in the United States as well.

According to Bush, therefore, "a fight to save the civilized world and values common to the West, to Asia, [and] to Islam" most immediately defines the new normalcy. The secular nature of the crusade thus anticipated in the name of that one inalienable freedom—freedom from fear—must be emphasized, but even such a broad understanding of the conflict may prove dangerously self-defeating. If the "fight" cannot be defined more specifically, no one is likely to ever win it explicitly because it might escalate endlessly and be pursued indefinitely. Yet, although terror is indivisible as a matter of common concern, terrorism as a question of individual perception remains divisible—between, say, Spain and Ireland, or Russia and Israel. "I'm a Christian," Bush told Chinese president Jiang Zemin on October 19, 2001. Meant as a statement of fact, designed to show "we feel confident discussing issues such as religion," this comment might be heard as a profession of faith, designed to justify and cement what the U.S. president had labeled a "crusade" a few weeks earlier.[6] "No government," Bush told his Chinese hosts, "should use our war against terrorism as an excuse to prosecute minorities within their borders." Understood as the corollary to his earlier doctrine—with us or with the terrorists—the warning would apply to many of the largest and most significant members of the September 11 coalitions, including Pakistan, Russia, and China.

Echoes of the Truman doctrine—an antiterrorist rhetoric initially based on comprehensible emotions—must be moderated. Otherwise, words that provide additional justification for a steady escalation of the U.S. war aims may ultimately isolate the United States from the coalition partners it still needs to defeat the enemies it still fears. Additionally, such rhetoric has unwanted consequences when other regional powers adopt the U.S. retaliatory model to fashion their own policies at home or abroad with a legitimacy that they lacked in earlier years.

Under conditions of new normalcy, countries that do not share, or even aim at, comparable values can nonetheless form a community of interest that leaves the coalition builder with many contradictions and related dilemmas. As the interest is broadly defined, the commitments it demands are rather diverse, and willing allies are grouped into variable coalitions that fulfill multiple missions: the will alone might not be enough in the absence of capabilities that are both relevant and necessary. Still, assuming that the mission determines the coalition, who will determine the mission if not the coalition builder itself?[7] This belief is neither a primitive form of unilateralism nor a renewed taste for multilateralism: the former could not sustain the broad community of interest the new normalcy uncovered, but the latter may stand in the way of the community of action needed to defend the shared interest against the new threat. It is a mixture—a sort of uni-multilateralism, whereby a power without peer acknowledges that it would rather not act without allies (assuming it could) whereas the allies—hardly limited to like-minded states and including a few potential foes—recognize that they cannot proceed without the peerless power (even assuming that they rather would).

Still the Indispensable Power

The new normalcy will be shaped by the Wars of 911, called thus not only to embody the ahistorical nature of a war launched allegedly on behalf of ideas that seemed to have their heyday before the first millennium had ended, but also because the war that started with a military campaign in Afghanistan is likely to continue elsewhere during the coming years, when it could even merge with other regional conflicts inherited from the Cold War. How these wars evolve will condition the U.S. role in the world in the following three ways.

First, the "Alliance of 911" was devised for the initial retaliatory campaign in and near Afghanistan. With the alliance designed not for show but for performance, the allies' role beside local Afghan groups was of little consequence to fulfill relatively limited military goals: topple the Taliban, dismantle Al Qaeda, and find Osama bin Laden.

The decision not to make this campaign into a Kosovo-like NATO war was justified in theory and clearly effective in practice. With fast-diminishing targets in Afghanistan, the air war was reduced to opportunity bombing that allowed little time for consultation with contributing allies, thereby reinforcing the need for a smaller alliance, which the covert nature of the ground war also made desirable. In Afghanistan, the alliance enlarged only when the campaign appeared to be ending and a larger peacekeeping force became necessary to manage the post-Taliban transition. Yet, although underutilized, the like-minded NATO allies that were both willing and capable, but not necessary, confirmed the marginal relevance of NATO as a community of action that is likely to remain the security institution of choice for the future—lest it changes substantially even as it expands significantly. In 2002 and beyond, other U.S.-led military campaigns required to win the Wars of 911 will not demand 100 percent followership from all.

Even under conditions of effective cooperation between the United States and the states of Europe, the centrality of U.S. power and leadership for the Wars of 911 has immediate consequences for the U.S. role in Europe. First, European allies will need to replace U.S. troops and assets currently deployed in Southeastern Europe as they are sent to fight new disorders elsewhere. Undoubtedly, U.S. troops will not return easily once withdrawn from any part of the Balkans, meaning that the "headline goal" that the European Union set for 2003, the development of a European Security and Defense Identity (ESDI), will emerge as a deadline for a discreet U.S. reappraisal of its involvement in the region. Finally, the new normalcy may be the catalyst for more U.S. support for ESDI, especially if the NATO countries can remain generally united in 2002 and as the U.S. need for a European counterpart in the Balkans is confirmed in 2003.

Under the conditions of new normalcy, the withdrawal of U.S. forces and the enhanced influence of European allies need not be viewed with concern. The post–September 11 trend for NATO points less to its marginalization than to its normalization: a whole, free, and strong Europe was the exit strategy devised on behalf of an alliance that was organized to prevent a recurrence of past instabilities in Central and Southeastern Europe, no less than to manage the emergence of new disorders in Eastern and even Northern Europe. As the EU pursues the postwar vision of the Truman administration for an ever larger part of the European continent, the events of September 11 help complete that vision by assisting Russia's move into the cooperative security community of NATO, even while Russia also finds space closer to the integrated economic community of the EU.

Next, the "Coalition of '89" is a post–Cold War antiterrorism coalition of affluent states needed for the rehabilitation of regions left devastated by the many decades of Cold War conflicts that were often waged at their expense. After September 11, the relative ease with which countries agreed to join the coalition confirms that they cannot afford to lose this war. Whether they can afford to win the war, however, remains to be seen. History reaps what it sows, even though those who live it never truly know what is being sown. Within the sole context of the Cold War, the unintended consequences—"blowbacks"—that have emerged during the past 10 years are considerable. Victory did not make the world safe for democracy. If anything, that part of the world that won, led by the United States, appears to be more immediately at risk than at any time during the past 50 years.

Afghanistan, as well as Pakistan, Somalia, Lebanon, Yemen, Sudan, and Iraq—to cite but a few plausible battlegrounds for the military campaign that started in October 2001—are parts of the territorial body count of the many wars waged during the past few decades, during and after the Cold War. To win these wars during the first half of the past century and to keep them limited during the century's second half, many aberrations were tolerated—ethnic cleansing, territorial partitions, economic exploitation, institutional collapse, societal decline or collapse, and much more. "Terrorism strikes at the innocent in order to draw attention to the sins of the invulnerable." If neglect is a sin, then the neglect of those parts of the world where the Cold War was fought was indeed sinful—whether these areas of neglect were about territorial divisions, social degradation, or economic collapse.[8] The Coalition of '89, organized in the context of the wide range of available multilateral institutions, must settle the formidable, unfinished business of the twentieth century. Some of that business is territorial, some political, some economic, and some a little more of a traditional security nature. None can be ignored, however, lest the war not be ended even after each of its military campaigns has been won. As stated by British minister for Europe Peter Hain, "Winning the peace is part of winning the war" lest the "seeds of terror" continue to grow in "the fertile soil of disaffection and distress."[9]

The Coalition of '89 also confirms the overhaul of the Bush administration's strategic thinking that began after Bush's election had been confirmed and that has accelerated since September 11. With failed states back in fashion, the nearly obsessive concern with ascending powers—especially China—has been fading. During the next few years, the Bush administration is likely to show more tolerance toward Beijing than might have been expected otherwise—from human rights to trade to third-country uses of launch facilities, among other things. Will China look the other way too; or will it grow restless as it watches with understandable concern as the United States penetrates East Asia further, improves its increasingly cozy relationship with Russia, and builds potentially closer relations with India? In short, with China as well, the United States has an opportunity to improve or worsen a bilateral relationship greatly, depending on the outcome of the Wars of 911 and the ways that outcome is achieved. Cooperating closely with a rising China sufficiently impressed by the conduct of the war and seeking accommodation even as China continues to rise to preeminence would be much better—but much worse to confirm China's fears of encirclement, which might result from the lasting deployment and ineffective use of U.S. forces in neighboring countries.

Finally, and perhaps most significantly, the events of September 11 have restored the legitimacy of force as the central pillar of a new international order that accommodates vital concerns of national security. Admittedly, after a difficult century of "total wars," the twenty-first century was not supposed to be entered this way. Yet, as the first year of the new century came to an end, the world faces three real prospects for major war among countries that find it difficult to control the deep hostilities they have fostered since they became independent (India and Pakistan, Israel and its neighbors) or since the Cold War ended (the United States and Iraq). In all these instances, the moderating presence of U.S. power as a rampart between the protagonists has faded, at least temporarily. Significantly, the governments in New Delhi and Tel Aviv use the same language as the United States. In coming months or years, other such examples may arise, as the model is tested in other regions where the unfinished business inherited from the past is plentiful and tolerance for resulting insecurities no longer so ample.

Faced with an unexpected new normalcy, the Bush administration has performed remarkably well. Arguably, the strategy it devised in a matter of weeks is the most comprehensive U.S. approach to the management of global disorders since the fateful weeks of 1947. As Michael Stürmer recalled, "containment" was envisioned as a strategy of economic reconstruction (Marshall Plan), political reconciliation (cooperative institutions), and regional security (NATO). Now, too, what is needed, and what is envisioned, is a comprehensive strategy built by the indispensable power as a coalition of coalitions designed to wage, win, and end not just one military campaign or one war but many wars—the Wars of 911.

Whether the Bush administration will show the patience and flexibility required for such an approach is not clear, especially if the U.S. public insists on periodic and measurable expressions of success in any of these wars and on visible allied solidarity during all of them. The test is yet to come—a test of will and a test of leadership. These tests are the same that many of the writers who attempted to have a glimpse of the United States' future "through the looking glass" anticipated before the events of September 11. For the most part, their pleas for the new U.S. administration seemed to be to stay engaged in the world (the test of will) but as an "enlightened superpower" that would not succumb to the twin sins of "complacency and arrogance."[10] In the summer of 2001, no one could have suspected that these tests would take the form that they have acquired since September 11. There is a new normalcy now, and its final form will very much depend on the U.S. role—a role that can no longer be avoided as a matter of might because of its power, but also as a matter of right because the United States was the first target of an intolerable form of global disorder.

Notes

1. The words cited are those of Akio Watanabe, "First among Equals," *The Washington Quarterly* 24, no. 3 (summer 2001): 75–81; Chong Guan Kwa and See Seng Tan, "The Keystone of World Order," *The Washington Quarterly* 24, no. 3 (summer 2001): 96–97; Mahmood Sariolghlam, "Justice for All," *The Washington Quarterly* 24, no. 3 (summer 2001): 118–121; Pascal Boniface, "The Specter of Unilateralism," *The Washington Quarterly* 24, no. 3 (summer 2001): 157–159; Peter Ludlow, "Wanted: A Global Partner," *The Washington Quarterly* 24, no. 3 (summer 2001): 163; Barry Rubin, "What Is Right Is in U.S. Interests," *The Washington Quarterly* 24, no. 3 (summer 2001): 127; Dmitri Trenin, "Less Is More," *The Washington Quarterly* 24, no. 3 (summer 2001): 135; Kanti Bajpai, "Add Five 'E's to Make a Partnership," *The Washington Quarterly* 24, no. 3 (summer 2001): 83.

2. For more on the Clinton legacy, see Simon Serfaty, "Memories of Leadership," *Brown Journal of World Affairs* 5, no. 2 (summer/fall 1998): 3–16.

3. "The New U.S. Challenge to Russia," *U.S. News and World Report*, May 30, 1977, p. 35 (interview with Zbigniew Brzezinski).

4. Bob Woodward, "CIA Told to Do Whatever Necessary to Kill Bin Laden," *Washington Post*, October 21, 2001, p. A22.

5. Robert D. Kaplan, *The Coming Anarchy: Shattering the Dreams of the Post–Cold War* (New York: Random House, 2000), p. 24. Putin is quoted in the *Washington Post*, October 9, 2001, p. A16.

6. Mike Allen, "Bush Says Terrorists Sought Markets' Ruin," *Washington Post*, October 21, 2001, p. A25.

7. "The greatest danger to the war on terrorism," concluded a recent editorial, "is not that the Bush administration will resort to unilateralism. It is that the United States will fail to act aggressively and creatively enough, over time, to break the current coalition apart." "The Coalition and the Mission," *Washington Post*, October 21, 2001, p. B6.

8. Chalmers Johnson, *Blowback: The Costs and Consequences of American Empire* (New York: Henry Holt, 2000), p. 33.

9. "Guardian-RUSI Conference," *Guardian*, October 31, 2000, p. 6.

10. Michael Stürmer, "Balance from Beyond the Sea," *The Washington Quarterly* 24, no. 3 (summer 2001): 147; Wu Ximbo, "To Be an Enlightened Superpower," *The Washington Quarterly* 24, no. 3 (summer 2001): 63; Watanabe, "First among Equals," p. 73.

What Does the World Want from America?

Michael J. Mazarr

Saved from Ourselves?

Perhaps the central principle of the philosophy of world politics known as realism—and surely the best known—is the concept of the "balance of power," which is not so much an injunction as the description of an iron law. National powers tend to balance, the theory holds, because individual states seek their own interests. Imperialists are opposed and eventually undermined. The intended victims of hegemons band together in self-defense. Aggressive, intrusive displays of power are ultimately self-limiting and, if they become extreme enough, self-destroying.

Long before the cooperative security movement took root among liberal defense analysts in the 1970s, realists were the first to become obsessed with the security dilemma—the idea that one state's efforts to defend itself could be seen by others as aggressive. Accordingly, classical, balance-of-power realism urges a preoccupation with limits, restraint, and prudence rather than brash displays of force.

When several nations "are obliged to deal with one another, there are only two possible outcomes," Henry Kissinger wrote. "Either one state becomes so strong that it dominates all the others and creates

Michael J. Mazarr is an adjunct professor of security studies at Georgetown University and cofounder of The Archigos Project, a nonprofit organization devoted to leadership training.

Copyright © 2002 by The Center for Strategic and International Studies and the Massachusetts Institute of Technology
The Washington Quarterly • 25:2 pp. 221–232.

an empire, or no state is ever quite powerful enough to achieve that goal. In the latter case, the pretensions of the most aggressive member of the international community are kept in check by a combination of the others, in other words, by the operation of a balance of power."[1] Even in a globalizing world, this basic principle remains true for Kissinger. Order, he insists, "will have to emerge much as it did in past centuries from a reconciliation and balancing of competing national interests."[2]

Before September 11, the United States was the world's dominant power and hegemon in need of balancing. Peter Rodman, President George W. Bush's assistant secretary of defense for international security affairs and formerly with the Nixon Center, wrote perceptively in 1999, "The extraordinary predominance that America now enjoys is a problem rather than a blessing. Most of the world's other major powers have made it into a central theme of their foreign policy to attempt to build counterweights to American power. This is, in fact, one of the main trends in international politics today."[3]

This trend is abundantly evident in the articles in the summer 2001 "Through the Looking Glass" section of *The Washington Quarterly*. The underlying theme of most of those essays is that U.S. power—at least the pushy, globalizing, post–Cold War version of it—needs rejustification so that it will not become self-defeating. The question now, after September 11, is whether a tragic historical event will inspire the United States to achieve precisely this goal.

U.S. Power under Assault

A reaction to U.S. power was undoubtedly well underway before September 11. From European grumblings over allegedly high-handed U.S. behavior in NATO, to energetic Russian and Chinese statements and efforts to unseat U.S. leadership on key issues, to resentment in the Americas over U.S. demands to "certify" countries as adequate belligerents in the "war" on drugs, much of the world was lining up in opposition to U.S. values and policies in ways not before seen.

Rodman's 1999 monograph *Uneasy Giant: The Challenges to American Predominance* catalogued this process. He cited the German newsweekly *Der Spiegel*: "The Americans are acting, in the absence of limits put to them by anybody or anything, as if they own a blank check in their 'McWorld.' ... America is now the Schwarzenegger of international politics: showing off muscles, obtrusive, intimidating." Rodman described French foreign minister Hubert Védrine's depiction of the United States as a "hyperpower." Védrine said that, because "there is no counterweight" to U.S. strength, a "risk of hegemony" existed, requiring France to contribute "to the emergence of several poles in the world capable of being a factor of equilibrium."[4]

The same line of thought runs through nearly all the essays in "Through the Looking Glass." Maria Claudia Drummond worries that the Free Trade Area of the Americas proposal "might have been devised to benefit only U.S. interests."[5] Wu Xinbo relates China's concerns about unbalanced U.S. influence; the United States, he says, neglects to "show respect to, and consideration for, the national feelings of others. Washington tends to seek absolute security for itself but is inclined to dismiss the legitimate security concerns of other countries." Pointedly, he refers to the growing "Chinese-Russian partnership" which has, he claims, become "more substantive over the past several years in response to perceived aggressiveness by the United States in Asia and Europe."[6] From Paris, Pascal Boniface explains that France must urge Washington to "heed the opinions (or at least the existence) of other nations" and reminds readers that, on issues from gun control to unilateral bullying in foreign policy, admiration for the United States "is not universal."[7]

The coalescence of opinion against the United States within the Arab world was as obvious before September 11 as it is afterward. Iran's Mahmood Sariolghalam emphasizes that "[t]he most significant U.S. challenge in the Middle East may be to reshape its policies and to improve the U.S. image in the Arab world. ... During the last decade, Arab perceptions and views of the United States have sharply deteriorated."[8]

Such opinions partly reflect balance-of-power realpolitik. Yet, for all the insights of balance-of-power theory, the world has been transformed since the archetypal, eighteenth-century maneuvering of European powers. What was underway before September 11 was not just a reaction to a great power; that interpretation does an injustice to the depth of the historical transformation underway. The United States is not just a great power. It is also the engine, and prime enforcer, of the globalization process. For good or for ill, a growing global chorus has conflated globalization with Americanization and is shaking an angry fist at both.

Some years ago, the political scientist Stephen Walt made an important contribution to balance-of-power theory. He modified the basic dictum by noting that not all power is created equal—not all states are aggressive or expansionist. States, Walt contended, balance against threats, not merely power; even a relatively weak state with big ambitions can produce more balancing than a massive one devoted to the status quo.[9] Armed with this distinction, one might wonder who would choose to balance against the United States, which is, after all, a satisfied, status quo, nonaggressive power and certainly not an immediate threat to anyone, at least not in classical military terms.

Yet, the United States is a threat in even more important terms—social and economic. The quintessential realist Hans Morgenthau, one of whose central beliefs was in the predominance of political-military power over all other forms, recognized the potential decisiveness of a very specific form of imperialism:

> Cultural imperialism is the most subtle and, if it were ever to succeed by itself alone, the most successful of imperialistic policies. ... If one could imagine the culture and, more particularly, the political ideology ... of State A conquering the minds of all the citizens determining the policies of State B, State A would have won a more complete victory and would have founded its supremacy on more stable grounds than any military conqueror or economic master.[10]

One could hardly find a better description of the practical effects of globalization. In countries around the world, many consider globalization a threat to their values, jobs, and ways of life. They view globalization as U.S.-led, U.S.-directed, and most beneficial to U.S. interests and companies. In responding to, or "balancing" against, that threat, they react to U.S. power as well.

Before September 11, the United States seemed to take the nexus between U.S. power and globalization less seriously than it now appears it must. John Ikenberry, for example, hopes for a benign U.S. hegemony as a product of the United States' willingness to create global institutions that check our power because they also restrain others.[11] The bottom line of his sophisticated analysis is that multilateralism is the best long-term route to self-interest. Yet, even this sensible strategy can itself become counterproductive if others perceive the institutions the United States creates in the name of multilateralism as arbiters and accelerators of a runaway globalization that primarily benefits the United States.

The Overriding Security Threat

As Thomas Friedman, a leading chronicler of globalization, has said, part of the challenge to U.S. policy is that globalization is a system, not just a catch-phrase. It makes very specific demands of countries, particularly developing ones, that institutions such as the International Monetary Fund, the World Bank, and the World Trade Organization enforce. Globalization boasts an ever-denser network of norms and procedures and rules. It has an ethos (consumerism) and a political analogue (representative democracy). In other words, globalization is a homogenous, hegemonic system, precisely that against which states have habitually balanced. Balancing against history, however, is difficult; swapping out the name and calling the same process "Americanization," to lay the blame on a specific nation, people, and government, is far easier. Of course, Osama bin Laden has done this, and, though he is thankfully almost unique in the degree of his fanaticism, he is part of a large and growing worldwide consensus on the basic point: that U.S. influence must be diluted.

Certainly, what bin Laden really wants, what he and his key lieutenants really believe, cannot be known for sure. He could be an entirely political actor in the realpolitik mold, worried about U.S. force projection in the Middle East. Far more likely is that his public statements reflect his real worldview—a dread at the cultural and religious onslaught of modernism and globalization. Fundamentalism "is beleaguered tradition. It is tradition defended in the traditional way—by reference to ritual truth—in a globalizing world that asks for reasons."[12] Violence in defense of tradition becomes necessary when it is under attack, only, today, in the context of globalization.

Before September 11, considering this line of thinking to be contrived and carrying few troubling implications for the United States, its security, and power was still possible, but no longer. The United States is well on the way to becoming the scapegoat for globalization's ills, a role for which other developed nations seem only too happy to nominate it. No serious thinking about long-term U.S. security can overlook the connection any longer. Friedman saw this development emerging two years ago in the brief, prescient section in *The Lexus and the Olive Tree* dealing with terrorism. Referring specifically to bin Laden and his followers, Friedman wrote that "the real, immediate national security threat to the United States in the twenty-first century" was what he called "the Super-Empowered Angry Man. ... The gravest danger that the United States faces today is from super-empowered individuals who hate America more than ever because of globalization and who can do something about it on their own, more than ever, thanks to globalization."[13]

For this reason, the United States needs not just blatantly self-interested foreign and defense policies, but also a hardheaded and legitimately multilateral and altruistic sensibility—not out of goodwill or a rush to world government, but out of clear-eyed self-interest. It now has an opportunity to embrace such a course because the terrorist attacks represented a grave irony: they were both the ultimate manifestation of, and perhaps the first step in the creation of an antidote to, antiglobalizationism dressed up as anti-Americanism. Thanks to bin Laden and his followers, the exploding global resentment of globalization with a U.S. face has been interrupted, if only briefly. Terrorism has generated a surge of nostalgic sympathy for the United States and given a bad name to those who would tear it down. The question is what the United States will do with this hiatus.

If the world is globalizing; if the United States is permanently, and increasingly, associated with that trend; if the attacks of September 11 are a warning that the forces in the world troubled by both occurrences are becoming more violent in their response, then the U.S. response to that tragic day must encompass more than x-ray machines for airports, bomb-sniffing robots, and shadowy special operations. It must address the larger trends at work, and it must do so by reemphasizing restraint, humility, serious multilateral consultation, and compromise, even as it asserts and defends its national interests.

The False Promise of Hegemony

Some wish that this requirement for multilateralism was a mirage and urge a cartoon version of tough-guy global arrogance—even more so after September 11 than before it. The standard-bearers of the hegemonic movement remain outside government; writers such as William Kristol and Robert Kagan, for example, invite impassioned and aggressive blows at nearly everyone who has the temerity to question U.S. power. Those who favor U.S. supremacy advocate "a U.S. foreign policy of maximum muscularity. No concession is offered to the traditional arts of diplomacy."[14]

Kagan's and Kristol's basic line is straightforward. Equating the present moment to the time when the 1970s "Committee on the Present Danger" warned of U.S. weakness during the Cold War, they write:

> The present danger is that the United States, the world's dominant power on whom the maintenance of international peace and the support of liberal democratic principles depends, will shrink from its responsibilities as the world's dominant power and—in a fit of absentmindedness, or parsimony, or indifference—will allow the international order that it sustains to collapse. The present danger is one of declining strength, flagging will, and confusion about our role in the world.[15]

Kagan's and Kristol's position on alliances is paradoxical in a manner that would enshrine recent U.S. arrogance as official foreign policy strategy. Being "with our allies" means promising to defend them, not to listen to them. The columnists advocate a strikingly paternalistic form of leadership in which Washington lets everyone know what is in their best interests and the leaders of other countries, shrugging and smiling wanly, acknowledge that, after all, Washington knows best. What happens, though, when U.S. allies are the ones who want U.S. power moderated, as Peter Ludlow and Boniface describe in their "Looking Glass" essays? What happens when allies object to U.S. efforts on their behalf, such as missile defenses or export controls? Kagan and Kristol counsel us not to worry. "Much of the current international attack on American 'hegemonism' is posturing."[16] Perhaps. As we learned to our horror on September 11, some of it is not.

Charles Krauthammer also does not seem very concerned about the hazard of the world declining to view the United States as a benevolent hegemon. In June 2001, he wrote with admiration about the Bush administration's "new foreign policy": unilateralism. This government, Krauthammer declared, was finally "willing to assert American freedom of action and the primacy of American national interests." Rather than "contain American power within a vast web of constraining international agreements, the new unilateralism seeks to strengthen American power and unashamedly deploy it on behalf of *self-defined* global ends." The goal is to "reassert American freedom of action."[17] This strategy may seem tempting, but one wonders what Krauthammer would think if a Russian or a Chinese or (worse still) a North Korean official said the same. One can imagine the headlines: "China's New Doctrine Threatens to Ditch Global Accords." Muscle flexing is fine as long as the United States is the one doing it.

As Al Gore's former national security aide Leon Fuerth has written, the "complacent view of U.S. trustworthiness" in which "one assumes that all the rest of the world, friends and enemies alike, have merely to hear what U.S. intentions are, and they will be reconciled,"[18] or the claim that everybody else knows in the end that the United States is not a threat, cannot withstand scrutiny. When the United States flexes, others will react; the result might not be as amenable to our interests or safety as the initial flexing seemed to be. This statement is, again, even more true because of the historical moment, which has lashed the United States firmly to the objective historical process of globalization. A very real, very powerful global dialogue about ways of blunting and undermining U.S. power was underway before September 11. A few of the hegemonists betray the realpolitiker's usual fidelity to Thucydides and his theories of human fallibility and the permanence of warfare and brutality. Thucydides' central theme, however—that Athens's over-bearing, rising power all but invited Sparta to launch a preemptive war—can also be read as a powerful argument for skepticism at any attempts to preserve U.S. primacy. Trying to do so would transform the United States into the twenty-first century Athens of the saga. Thucydides has already told us how that story ends.

At the outset, the new Bush administration was theoretically equipped to understand the risks of primacy, but in practice—perhaps because it had to stand its ground in its early months on a handful of demonstrably bad treaties—it behaved in strikingly unilateral fashion. It seemed unwilling to give up the temptation to dictate, hector, and bully that characterized U.S. foreign policy during President Bill Clinton's years in office. The administration appended to that overbearing style the repudiation of a parade of multilateral agreements: the Kyoto global warming accord, the International Criminal Court, the Biological Weapons Convention protocol, and the Anti-Ballistic Missile Treaty, among others. By September 10, 2001, events appeared headed for a bitter intensification of the already explosive debate over U.S. power.

A Brief Window of Opportunity

On September 11, in the span of an hour, the United States went from being the omnipotent bully to the pathetic victim—the victim of a form of terrorism that threatens many other states as well. The events of that day raise some big questions. Could worldwide sympathy for the

United States help mask, or even reverse, the hostile reactions to globalization and its leading advocate and symbolic pilot? Could the worldwide campaign against terror bring the commonalities of globalizing, developed states to the fore and submerge their differences over emerging global norms?[19] Arguing for globalization against idealistic, selfless unions or cultural icons and environmentalists, amid mountains of evidence of inequality, social upheaval, and ecological devastation that "progress" has wrought, is one thing. The debate changes when the United States and its allies are pit against terrorists.

An urgent, global terrorist threat could drive the world's great powers into a dialogue on more forceful mutual values and rules. U.S. interactions with allies, friends, and others could create new expectations and norms. Such a process will not erase contrary perceptions, but it will lay more seeds of commonality in the face of a mutually feared threat. Kissinger, the quintessential realpolitiker, believes that such a shift may be underway:

> The attack on the United States has produced an extraordinary congruence of interests among the major powers. None wants to be vulnerable to shadowy groups that have emerged, from Southeast Asia to the edge of Europe. Few have the means to resist alone. The NATO allies have ended the debate about whether, after the Cold War, there is still a need for an Atlantic security structure. Our Asian allies, Japan and Korea, being democratic and industrialized, share this conviction. India, profoundly threatened by domestic Islamic fundamentalism, has much to lose by abandoning a common course. Russia perceives a common interest due to its contiguous Islamic southern regions. China shares a similar concern with respect to its western regions.

"Paradoxically," Kissinger concludes, "terrorism has evoked a sense of world community that has eluded theoretical pleas for world order." He refers to an "extraordinary opportunity that has come about to recast the international system."[20] Recast it, indeed: cast the United States in a new role, one defined by its perceived willingness to abide by a collectively shaped globalization and to do much more than it has been doing to underwrite a sustainable, equitable, and healthy version of it.

One has to admit (as Kissinger surely would) that the odds remain against any sort of radical transformation spurred by the threat of terrorism. The "war on terrorism" seems increasingly likely to be a very brief, narrowly targeted military affair followed by years of grinding law enforcement operations. Yet, the opportunity is real. Handled properly, the response to terrorism could build on the sympathy these attacks sparked for the United States, demonstrate a true U.S. respect for coalition decisionmaking, and jump-start global efforts to dampen the effects of globalization-cum-Americanization. This outcome is not preordained; inasmuch as it depends on statesmanship with a long view and a light hand, it remains unlikely. Handled poorly, the U.S. response could exacerbate problems that it now has a chance to curb. The risks to the United States of its overweening power and its close association with the costs that globalization imposes became obvious in September 2001. Ultimately, the best form of "homeland security" will be a policy designed to ease these twin dangers.

What to Do?

Of course, the United States can hardly solve the problem of globalization's real and perceived costs, but "solving" it is not the point. The existence of a few thousand people around the globe who are dedicated to undermining U.S. power in violent ways is one thing. Large portions of key societies turning against the United States and the global values of free trade and free society that it represents is quite another. If the United States can win the sympathy of the majority of the population of key countries—from Pakistan to Malaysia, Russia to France—it can ultimately blunt the terror that Bush has called the "new 'ism'" in world politics. Doing so, however, against the background of the resentment that had built up before September 11 will take much effort—effort that was not underway in the slightest degree before the attacks. As horrible as the sight of aircraft flying into the World Trade Center towers was and remains, that lingering image will not be enough to forestall a new surge of anti-Americanism. Only sensible policies can do that.

The paradoxical lesson of terror is that U.S. power, mightily and brutally challenged, must respond by becoming more generous, humble, restrained, and collaborative. The United States must lead by inclusion and compromise rather than by fiat. It must act—and be seen to act—to ease the hard social and economic edges of globalization that so many around the world view as a U.S. creation. The United States must rejustify its power in the eyes of much of the world—an effort that will determine whether, over time, history views terrorists such as bin Laden as a nuisance to the United States and globalization or a deadly threat.

What would such an effort look like? The "Through the Looking Glass" essays are instructive. The authors' advice (where it is global and not strictly bilateral) falls into two broad categories: work collaboratively while treating others with respect and lead the world vigorously toward a more benign version of globalization. Drummond points to "the importance of approaching negotiations, no matter how asymmetrical the partners, in a spirit of consultation and equality. Unity is not possible if diversity is not recognized and respected." At the same time, the "spaceship called Earth desperately needs a captain and a vision of the route."[21] Washington's response to this call could involve a number of obvious steps—redoubling foreign aid, investing massively in renewable energy to address environmental concerns, finding ways to play a meaningful role in the dread requirement for "nation building" without exhausting the U.S. armed forces. Equally important, however, will be the style, diplomatic tone, and decisionmaking mechanisms within and outside the antiterror coalition. Can the United States compromise on important issues such as missile defense? Can it meaningfully consider the interests of others? In other words, can it conduct itself like a partner rather than a selfish outsider?

For reasons that become abundantly apparent in the "Through the Looking Glass" section, positive answers to these questions are hardly guaranteed. Some of the wishes of the United States' would-be partners run directly counter to perceived U.S. interests. When Dmitri Trenin reports on the growing desire of Russian elites to be left alone to run the war in Chechnya as they please and conduct their economic affairs as they will, he relays an attitude that would ask the United States to abandon all leverage on human rights and economic reform.[22] (In the bargain, Moscow demands that the United States commit itself to undertaking only military action specifically approved by the United Nations Security Council—in other words, by Russia itself. Had this demand been effective in 1999, genocide might still be underway in Kosovo.) Wu repeats the familiar Chinese assertion that the United States should gradually abandon a "large-scale, permanent military presence" in Asia, a step most U.S. analysts agree would make conflict more, not less, likely. Sariolghalam would like Washington to get tougher on undemocratic Arab states—perhaps a sensible long-term objective, but one with immense short-term risks.

U.S. policy, meanwhile, will remain—as it must and should—a mixture of multilateral compromise and unilateral leadership. The issue is not one of a black-and-white choice, but of balance between the two. The United States sometimes defends principles and values that others find uncomfortable. This principled leadership often has value, and straight-jacketing U.S. policy with a compulsion to always be multilateral would not serve U.S. interests or world peace and security. At least some of the accords that the Bush administration rejected in its so-called unilateralist frenzy happened to be pretty rotten deals, the ignore-developing-nations'-pollution Kyoto accord and the verification-challenged biological weapons protocol chief among them. The developments generate sympathy for the argument of Steven Miller, who sees no particular reason to believe that a United States at war against terror must be a United States in love with multilateralism.[23]

The leadership challenge is a paradoxical and therefore maddening one: to promote a specific vision of international security unapologetically and to defend sometimes selfish interests and values while leading collaboratively and altruistically. Arguably, our single most important national security currency is at stake: other nations' and peoples' perceptions of U.S. power. The "Looking Glass" essays offer a few examples of how to proceed with this task. Boniface and Ludlow, to cite one option, both nominate full and honest acceptance of a common European security policy as an easy win for U.S. multilateralism. Boniface points to the conduct of the 1999 military operations in Kosovo as another case in which Washington, perhaps grudgingly, took allied concerns into account. These events are the exceptions; the balance in U.S. policy, for the better part of a decade, has favored unilateralism and a narrow, short-term view of our interests to a dangerous degree.

The jury, such as it is, remains out but is watching carefully and will return its verdict during the next decade. From Pakistan to Malaysia, to Mexico and France, and a hundred other countries, those who have worried about U.S. power will recalculate and act accordingly. The overriding question for U.S. policy today that the insightful essays in "Through the Looking Glass" ask is, What arguments will we make in our defense after September 11?

Notes

1. Henry Kissinger, *Diplomacy* (New York: Simon and Schuster, 1994), p. 20.

2. Ibid., p. 805.

3. Peter Rodman, *Uneasy Giant: The Challenges to American Predominance* (Washington, D.C.: Nixon Center, 1999), p. 2.

4. Ibid., pp. 6, 9–10.

5. Maria Claudia Drummond, "Guide Globalization into a Just World Order," *The Washington Quarterly* 24, no. 3 (summer 2001): 178–179.

6. Wu Xinbo, "To Be an Enlightened Superpower," *The Washington Quarterly* 24, no. 3 (summer 2001): 63, 69.

7. Pascal Boniface, "The Specter of Unilateralism," *The Washington Quarterly* 24, no. 3 (summer 2001): 157.

8. Mahmood Sariolghalam, "Justice for All," *The Washington Quarterly* 24, no. 3 (summer 2001): 115.

9. Stephen Walt, *The Origins of Alliances* (Ithaca: Cornell University Press, 1990).

10. Hans J. Morgenthau, *Politics among Nations: The Struggle for Power and Peace (Brief Edition)*, revised by Kenneth W. Thompson (New York: McGraw Hill, 1993), p. 72.

11. John Ikenberry, *After Victory* (Princeton: Princeton University Press, 2000).

12. Anthony Giddens, *Runaway World* (New York: Routledge, 2000), p. 67.

13. Thomas Friedman, *The Lexus and the Olive Tree* (New York: Random House, 2000), p. 398.

14. Jonathan Clarke, "The Guns of 17th Street," *National Interest* (spring 2001): 104.

15. William Kristol and Robert Kagan, "Introduction: National Interest and Global Responsibility," in *Present Dangers: Crisis and Opportunity in American Foreign and Defense Policy*, Kagan and Kristol, eds. (San Francisco: Encounter Books, 2000), p. 4.

16. Ibid., p. 22.

17. Charles Krauthammer, "The New Unilateralism," *Washington Post*, June 8, 2001, p. A29 (emphasis added).

18. Leon Fuerth, "Return of the Nuclear Debate," *The Washington Quarterly* 24, no. 4 (autumn 2001): 100.

19. Part of the argument in this section mirrors some of the thinking in John Ikenberry, "American Grand Strategy in the Age of Terror," *Survival* 43 (winter 2001–2002).

20. Henry Kissinger, "Where Do We Go from Here?" *Washington Post*, November 6, 2001, sec. A, p. 23.

21. Drummond, "Guide Globalization into a Just World Order," pp. 175, 179.

22. Dmitri Trenin, "Less Is More," *The Washington Quarterly* 24, no. 3 (summer 2001): 136–137, 143–144.

23. Steven E. Miller, "The End of Unilateralism or Unilateralism Redux?" *The Washington Quarterly* 25, no. 1 (winter 2002): 15–29.

Christopher Layne

Offshore Balancing Revisited

In the wake of September 11, saying that everything has changed has be-come fashionable. Yet, although much indeed has changed, some im-portant things have not. Before September 11, U.S. hegemony (or primacy, as some call it) defined the geopolitical agenda. It still does. Indeed, the attack on the United States and the subsequent war on ter-rorism waged by the United States underscore the myriad ways in which U.S. hegemony casts its shadow over international politics. The fundamental grand strategic issues that confronted the United States before September 11 are in abeyance temporarily, but the expansion of NATO, the rise of China, and ballistic missile defense have not disap-peared. In fact, the events of September 11 have rendered the deeper question these issues pose—whether the United States can, or should, stick to its current strategy of maintaining its post–Cold War hegemony in international politics—even more salient.

Hegemony is the term political scientists use to denote the over-whelming military, economic, and diplomatic preponderance of a single great power in international politics. To illustrate the way in which U.S. hegemony is the bridge connecting the pre–September 11 world to the post–September 11 world, one need only return to the "Through the

Christopher Layne is an associate professor in the School of International Studies at the University of Miami.

Copyright © 2002 by The Center for Strategic and International Studies and the Massachusetts Institute of Technology
The Washington Quarterly • 25:2 pp. 233–248.

Looking Glass" collection of articles in the summer 2001 issue of *The Washington Quarterly*. A unifying theme runs through those articles: the authors' acknowledgment of U.S. primacy and their ambivalent responses about it.

Collectively, the "Through the Looking Glass" contributors make an important point about U.S. power that policymakers in Washington do not always take to heart: U.S. hegemony is a double-edged sword. In other words, U.S. power is a paradox. On one hand, U.S. primacy is acknowledged as the most important factor in maintaining global and regional stability. "[I]f not for the existing security framework provided by bilateral and multilateral alliance commitments borne by the United States, the world could, or perhaps would, be a more perilous place."[1] On the flip side of the coin, many—indeed most—of the contributors evince resentment at the magnitude of U.S. power and fear about how Washington exercises that power.

China, specifically, wants the United States to accommodate its rise to great-power status and stop interfering in the Taiwan issue. The political elite in Moscow wants Washington to treat Russia like a great power equal to the United States and stop meddling in Russia's domestic affairs.[2] Warnings are issued that for its own good—and the world's—the United States must change its ways and transform itself into a benign, or "enlightened," superpower. As the contributions to "Through the Looking Glass" demonstrate, the paradox of U.S. power evokes paradoxical reactions to it. U.S. primacy is "bad" when exercised unilaterally or to justify "isolationist" policies, but U.S. hegemony is "good" when exercised multilaterally to advance common interests rather than narrow U.S. ones.[3]

U.S. Power: The Effects of September 11

The paradox of U.S. power has been very much on display since September 11. U.S. primacy in the war on terrorism has its benefits. First, unrivaled U.S. military power is obviously a plus. In terms of military capabilities, the United States indeed enjoys what the Pentagon calls "full spectrum dominance." Today, the United States can war against virtually any foe, whether big powers, rogue states, or terrorist groups, and prevail on the battlefield at little or no cost. Second, because of its preponderant military and economic power, the United States has been able to organize an international coalition against terrorism. Only an enormously powerful state—a true hegemon—could make stick its admonition to the rest of the world that you are either with us or with the terrorists.

No doubt, President George W. Bush's "us or them" declaration carried an implicit element of threat. Certainly, the United States has many sticks to wield. Being a hegemon, however, also means that the United States has plenty of carrots to use as coalition-building inducements. By making "side payments"—the political science jargon for what most would call bribes—Washington, for example, was able to draw a reluctant Pakistan into its antiterror coalition. The United States would have been hard pressed to project its military power into Afghanistan without the use of Pakistan's bases and airspace, but Pakistan's open alignment with the United States was anything but a slam-dunk. After all, for Islamabad, Afghanistan holds crucial strategic importance. Pakistan's need to have a friendly government in control of Kabul explains its pre–September 11 support for the Taliban. At the same time, Pakistan's archenemy, India, backed the anti-Taliban Northern Alliance. When you throw into the mix factors such as ethnic kinship (like the Taliban and much of the rest of southern Afghanistan, many Pakistanis are Pashtuns) and Pakistan's tenuous domestic political situation (where support for Islamic fundamentalism purportedly is widespread), the government of Pakistani president Pervez Musharraf had many compelling reasons to distance itself from the United States.[4]

Washington was well positioned to overcome Pakistan's ambivalence about joining the coalition because the United States had a well-stocked bag of diplomatic and economic goodies into which it could reach to bestow rewards on Islamabad for Pakistani cooperation. For one, the United States was able to tell Pakistan that it would lift the economic sanctions it had earlier imposed as punishment for Pakistan's nuclear weapons testing. The United States also has promised impoverished Pakistan some $600 million a year in foreign aid for the next two years, plus other economic and trade inducements.[5] Moreover, although the International Monetary Fund (IMF) is not supposed to assist states for political reasons, it has done precisely that in Pakistan's case.[6] The IMF's decision to reward Pakistan for joining the U.S.-led coalition is in itself another example of U.S. hegemonic power. In international institutions such as the IMF, U.S. power is preponderant, and the United States alone is able to use these institutions to advance its geopolitical interests.

The downside of U.S. power also has been evident since September 11. Given the horrific nature of the September 11 attacks, traditional U.S. security partners such as NATO (and especially Great Britain) rallied strongly to the U.S. side. In many ways, especially in the areas of intelligence cooperation and crackdowns on Europe-based terror cells, U.S. allies have made significant contributions to the war on terrorism. Yet, at the same time, NATO clearly has tried at the governmental level to constrain the exercise of U.S. power, as demonstrated by early admonitions for the United States to obtain United Nations (UN) authorization to use military force in Afghanistan; by pleas for the United States to limit its bombing of Afghanistan; and, perhaps most important, in warnings that Washington should not expand the geographical scope of the war on terrorism, for example, by going after Iraq.[7] At the level of public opinion, at least in the war's early stages, a significant number of Europeans opposed the U.S. campaign and openly expressed hostility toward U.S. hegemony itself.[8]

In Russia, before President Vladimir Putin decided to cast Moscow's lot with Washington, the highest decisionmaking levels were apparently split on whether Russia should welcome or oppose a U.S. military presence in the former Soviet republics of Central Asia. The dissenters on this point in Moscow were fearful that U.S. use of Central Asian bases to prosecute the war in Afghanistan would become the opening wedge to establishing a permanent U.S. presence in the region. In the Islamic world, fear and resentment of U.S. power was more pronounced. Even key U.S. client states such as Saudi Arabia and Egypt only circum-spectly supported the U.S. military effort, and their own contributions to the war effort were minimal. Not unexpectedly, on the Arab and Is-lamic "street," hostility both to the war, especially U.S. bombing of Af-ghanistan, and to U.S. hegemony was widespread. (The volatile nature of public opinion mostly explains the tepid support for the United States extended by Saudi Arabia, Egypt, and others in the region.) In essence, although the coalition held together through the campaign in Afghanistan, the war on terrorism evoked a spectrum of responses to U.S. power, ranging from unease (NATO) to real hostility (the Persian Gulf/Middle East region).

Stepping Back to See the View

Given the paradox of U.S. power, what should U.S. policymakers make of perceptions of U.S. hegemony, and how should Washington respond to these perceptions? To answer these questions, one should step back from ongoing events and put the issue of U.S. hegemony in a broader perspective. Obviously, by transforming the international system from its post-1945 bipolarity to unipolarity, the Soviet Union's collapse el-evated the United States to a historically unprecedented position of primacy in international politics. Although the Cold War's end did not trigger a "great debate" about U.S. grand strategy, it did elicit a discus-sion about grand strategy among foreign policy analysts and scholars of strategic studies.[9] Contributors to this conversation have adopted U.S. post–Cold War hegemony as a common starting point. The questions they have asked concern whether the current unipolar distribution of power is stable and whether the United States should deliberately seek to maintain its preponderance in the international political system.

Policymakers and scholars of strategic studies widely agree that power plays a central role in international politics. If power counts, then embracing the proposition that the United States should seek to amass as much power as it possibly can is not a great leap of faith. Con-sequently, the United States should do everything possible to maintain its current hegemony, which has been the goal of U.S. grand strategy for more than a decade. If the duchess of Windsor had been a U.S. strategist, she would have said that the United States could never be too rich, too well armed, or too powerful. Under the administrations of George H. W. Bush, Bill Clinton, and George W. Bush, the overriding aim of U.S. grand strategy has been to ensure that the United States maintains its lofty geopolitical perch by preventing the rise of new great powers (or the resurgence of old ones, such as Russia) that could challenge the United States as king of the hill. (In Pentagon-speak, such powers are called "peer competitors.") In other words, U.S. grand strategy has sought for the last decade the indefinite prolongation of what one commentator called the United States' "unipolar moment."[10]

Today, the United States apparently has firmly consolidated its global hegemony. Surely, no great power in the history of the modern international system (since approximately 1500) has ever been as dominant as the United States in global politics. Still, history suggests a note of caution is appropriate. The United States is merely the most recent great power to seek hegemony. When examining the fates of previous hegemonic contenders, a clear lesson emerges: aspiring to hegemony or even attaining it for a short period of time is different than maintaining it.

Although at first the conclusion may appear counterintuitive, states that seek hegemony invariably end up being less, not more, secure. Being powerful is good in international politics, but being too powerful is not. The reasoning behind this axiom is straightforward as well as the geopolitical counterpart to the law of physics that holds that, for every action, there is an equal and opposite reaction. Simply put, the response to hegemony is the emergence of countervailing power. Because international politics is indeed a competitive, "self-help" system, when too much power is concentrated in the hands of one state, others invariably fear for their own security. Each state fears that a hegemon will use its overwhelming power to aggrandize itself at that state's expense and will act defensively to offset hegemonic power. Thus, one of hegemony's paradoxes is that it contains the seeds of its own destruction.

This insight is not merely abstract academic theorizing but is confirmed by an ample historical record. Since the beginning of the modern international system, a succession of bids have been made for hegemony: the Habsburg Empire under Charles V, Spain under Philip II, France under Louis XIV as well as Napoleon, and Germany under Hitler (and, some historians would argue—although the point is contested—under Wilhelm II). None of these attempts to gain hegemony succeeded. Why did these hegemonic contenders fail?

First, although not actually great powers, one or more states throughout most of international history have clearly been candidates for that status because of their latent power. The threat posed to their security by a rising hegemon has served as the catalyst for these candidates to adopt the necessary policies to mobilize their resources and transform their latent power into actual great-power capabilities. Two prior "unipolar moments" in international history illustrate this point. When France under Louis XIV briefly attained hegemony in Europe, both England and Austria rose from candidate status to great-power status and used their newly acquired capabilities to end France's geopolitical preeminence. Similarly, England's mid-nineteenth-century global preponderance (the fabled Pax Britannica) spurred the United States, Germany, and Japan to emerge as great powers, largely to offset British supremacy. In each of these instances, for reasons of self-defense, states that were candidate great powers were impelled to come forward and emerge as full-fledged great powers in order to ensure that they would not fall victim to the reigning hegemon.[11]

Second, hegemons invariably are defeated because other states in the international system, frequently spearheaded by newly emerged great powers, form counterbalancing coalitions against them. Thus, the English and the Dutch defeated Philip II. Various coalitions anchored by Holland, the newly emerged great powers of England and Austria, and an established great power in Spain undid Louis the XIV. A coalition composed of England, Russia, Austria, and Prussia rebuffed Napoleon's bid for hegemony. Instead of war, the enervating economic effects of trying to maintain primacy against the simultaneous chal-

What Does the World Want from America?

lenges of the United States, Russia, France, and Germany undermined British hegemony in the nineteenth century. The wartime grand alliance of the United States, Great Britain, and the Soviet Union defeated Hitler.

Commenting on this historical record, Henry Kissinger has rightly observed, "Hegemonic empires almost automatically elicit universal resistance, which is why all such claimants sooner or later exhausted themselves."[12] A simple fact explains this pattern: left unbalanced, hegemonic power threatens the security of the other major states in the international system. In the first few decades of the twenty-first century, U.S. primacy will likely prompt the same response that previous hegemonic aspirants provoked: new great powers will emerge to offset U.S. power, and these new great powers will coalesce to check U.S. hegemonic ambitions.

Is the United States Different?

Nothing suggests that the United States will be exempt from the tendency of others to contest its global preeminence. Yet, in the latest twist on "American exceptionalism," U.S. strategists apparently do believe "it won't happen to us." They think that the United States is a qualitatively different type of hegemon: a "benevolent" hegemon whose "soft power" immunizes it against a backlash, that is, its liberal democratic ideology and culture make it attractive to others. U.S. policymakers also believe that others do not fear U.S. geopolitical preeminence because they believe that the United States will use its unprecedented power to promote the common good of the international system rather than to advance its own selfish aims. As then–national security adviser Sandy Berger put it:

> We are accused of dominating others, of seeing the world in zero-sum terms in which any other country's gain must be our loss. But that is an utterly mistaken view. It's not just because we are the first global power in history that is not an imperial power. It's because for 50 years we have consciously tried to define and pursue our interests in

a way that is consistent with the common good—rising prosperity, expanding freedom, [and] collective security.[13]

U.S. strategists may believe that others view U.S. hegemony this way, but the "others" do not—a point clearly evident in the articles in "Through the Looking Glass."

Well before September 11, indeed throughout most of the past decade, a strong undercurrent of unease on the part of other states about the imbalance of power in the United States' favor has existed. This simmering mistrust of U.S. power burst into the open during the final years of the Clinton administration. Russia, China, India, and even European allies such as France and Germany feared that the United States was unilaterally seeking to maintain its global military dominance. As history would lead us to expect, others responded to U.S. hegemony by concerting their efforts against it. Russia and China, long estranged, found common ground in a nascent alliance that opposed U.S. "hegemonism" by seeking to reestablish a multipolar world.

Similarly, U.S. European allies were openly expressing the view that something must be done geopolitically to rein in a too powerful United States. French president Jacques Chirac and his foreign minister, Hubert Védrine, gave voice to Europe's fears. Arguing that U.S. economic and military dominance is so formidable that the term "superpower" is inadequate to convey the true extent of U.S. preeminence, Védrine called the United States a "hyperpower" and added, "We cannot accept either a politically unipolar world, nor a culturally uniform world, nor the unilateralism of a single hyperpower. And that is why we are fighting for a multipolar, diversified, and multilateral world."[14]

Ironically, it was U.S. intervention in Kosovo that crystallized fears of U.S. hegemony. As a result, an incipient anti-U.S. alliance comprising China, Russia, and India began to emerge. Each of these countries viewed the U.S.-led intervention in Kosovo as a dangerous precedent establishing Washington's self-declared right to ignore the norm of international sovereignty and interfere in other states' internal affairs. The three states increased their military cooperation, especially with respect to arms transfers and the sharing of military technology, and, like the Europeans, declared their support for a "multipolar" world, that is, a world in which countervailing power offsets U.S. power. The Kosovo conflict—fought in part to validate NATO's post–Cold War credibility—had the perverse effect of dramatizing the dangerous disparity between U.S. and European geopolitical power. It prompted Europe to take its first serious steps to redress that power imbalance by acquiring through the European Defense and Security Policy (EDSP) the kinds of military capabilities it needs to act independently of the United States. If the European Union (EU) fulfills EDSP's longer-term goals, it will emerge as an independent strategic player in world politics. The clear objective of investing Europe with the capacity to brake U.S. hegemonic aspirations will have driven that emergence.

If any doubt remained that U.S. hegemony would trigger a nasty geopolitical "blowback," it surely was erased on September 11. The Middle East is an extraordinarily complex and volatile place in terms of its geopolitics, and the reaction there to U.S. hegemony is somewhat nuanced. Nothing, however, is subtle about the United States' hegemonic role in the Persian Gulf, a role that flows inexorably from the strategy of U.S. primacy. With the onset of the Persian Gulf War, the United States began to manage the region's security directly. The subsequent U.S. policy of "dual containment"—directed simultaneously against the region's two strategic heavyweights, Iran and Iraq—underscored the U.S. commitment to maintaining its security interests through a hegemonic strategy, rather than a strategy of relying on local power balances to prevent a hostile state from dominating the region or relying on other great powers to stabilize the Gulf and Middle East.

The U.S. role in the Gulf has rendered it vulnerable to a hegemonic backlash on several levels. First, some important states in the region (including Iran and Iraq) aligned against the United States because they resented its intrusion into regional affairs. Second, in the Gulf and the Middle East, the self-perception among both elites and the general public that the region has long been a victim of "Western imperialism" is widespread. In this vein, the United States is viewed as just the latest extraregional power whose imperial aspirations weigh on the region, which brings a third factor into play. Because of its interest in oil, the United States is supporting regimes—Saudi Arabia, Kuwait, and the Gulf emirates—whose domestic political legitimacy is contested. Whatever strategic considerations dictate that Washington prop up these regimes, that it does so makes the United States a lightning rod for those within these countries who are politically disaffected. Moreover, these regimes are not blind to the domestic challenges to their grip on power. Because they are concerned about inflaming public opinion (the much talked about "street"), both their loyalty and utility as U.S. allies are, to put it charitably, suspect. Finally, although U.S. hegemony is manifested primarily in its overwhelming economic and military muscle, the cultural dimension to U.S. preeminence is also important. The events of September 11 have brought into sharp focus the enormous cultural clash, which inescapably has overtones of a "clash of civilizations," between Islamic fundamentalism and U.S. liberal ideology.

The terrorism of Osama bin Laden results in part from this cultural chasm, as well as from more traditional geopolitical grievances. In a real sense, bin Laden's brand of terrorism—the most dramatic illustration of U.S. vulnerability to the kind of "asymmetric warfare" of which some defense experts have warned—is the counterhegemonic balancing of the very weak. For all of these reasons, the hegemonic role that the strategy of preponderance assigns to the United States as the Gulf's stabilizer was bound to provoke a multilayered backlash against U.S. predominance in the region. Indeed, as Richard K. Betts, an acknowledged expert on strategy, presciently observed several years ago, "It is hardly likely that Middle Eastern radicals would be hatching schemes like the destruction of the World Trade Center if the United States had not been identified so long as the mainstay of Israel, the shah of Iran, and conservative Arab regimes and the source of a cultural assault on Islam."[15] (Betts was referring to the 1993 attack on the World Trade Center.)

In the wake of U.S. diplomatic and battlefield success in the first phase of the war on terrorism, some doubtless will conclude that victory has erased the paradox of U.S. power. The United States, after all, stands at the zenith of its hegemonic power—militarily, diplomatically, economically, and culturally. When even potential rivals such as China and Russia have been folded into the U.S.-led coalition against terrorism, concluding that U.S. primacy is secure for a long, long time is tempting indeed. The outlook for U.S. primacy, however, may not be quite so rosy. Appearances can be deceiving, and the paradox of U.S. power remains.

Looking into the Crystal Ball

In the short term, if the United States expands the war on terrorism, especially by confronting Iraq and Saddam Hussein, fears of U.S. hegemony will resurface quickly. If the United States moves against Iraq, the fracture of its current coalition is a near certainty, with both NATO and Middle Eastern clients refusing to support the United States. In the longer term, even if the coalition holds together for a time (assuming that Washington foregoes attempting to oust Hussein), believing that the wartime coalition represents a permanent accommodation by others to U.S. hegemony would be unwise. To think otherwise is to misunderstand the nature of international politics.

The articles in "Through the Looking Glass" are a very good predictor of expected events, both in the war on terrorism and beyond. Other states remain profoundly uneasy about U.S. primacy and, to rein in the United States, will step up calls for Washington to act multilaterally rather than unilaterally. The reasoning is simple: they want to constrain U.S. power by pressuring the United States to refrain from taking actions that the coalition, formal alliances such as NATO, and international institutions such as the UN do not sanction. Their desire to bind U.S. power in a web of multilateral restraints is understandable, but the United States must retain its capacity for acting unilaterally in defense of its national interests. At the same time, to avoid triggering counter-hegemonic blowback, the United States must act with self-restraint.

Considering whether the United States should act unilaterally or multilaterally involves a false dichotomy. In international politics, great powers always put their self-interest first; they must. International politics is an especially competitive realm, as Realist scholars of international politics have argued since the time of Thucydides's *History of the Peloponnesian Wars*. In the jargon of international relations scholars, international politics is an "anarchic" system because no central authority makes and enforces laws and maintains order. Consequently, international politics is also a self-help system in which each actor must rely primarily on its own efforts to ensure its survival and security and in which each can employ the means of its choice, including force, to advance its interests. "States operating in a self-help world almost always act according to their own self-interest and do not subordinate their interests to the interests of other states, or to the interests of the so-called international community. The reason is simple: it pays to be selfish in a self-help world."[16] The nature of international politics impels great powers to think of themselves first; their natural inclination is to act unilaterally. Whether confronting Iraq or building a national missile defense, the United States should never subject policies that affect U.S. interests to multilateral processes that require others to acquiesce before Washington can act.

Unilateralism, the default strategy of great powers, does not mean that they should never cooperate or ally with other states. In alliances, however, a great power must never lose sight of some fundamental tenets of international politics. States that form alliances and coalitions typically have one common interest and many conflicting ones. The interest that binds together allies or coalition partners is the threat that a common adversary poses to the security of all. To defeat that threat, the other, divisive issues among alliance or coalition partners may be forced into the background, but they do not vanish. Even in wartime, coalition partners jockey to gain advantage in the postwar world. Occasionally, coalitions fissure during wartime because reconciliation of the partners' competing interests proves impossible. In any event, once the threat had been disposed, the glue binding an alliance or coalition surely dissolves, and the partners go their separate ways—the inevitable outcome in a self-help system.

In concrete terms today, Western Europe, China, Russia, and Japan are aligned with the United States to deal with the common threat of terrorism. Because the coalition partners have differing interests, the coalition may fragment if the United States acts unilaterally to expand the war on terrorism. Even if the coalition should hold together until the war on terrorism is terminated, the conflicting geopolitical interests that divide the United States and its partners will then surely resurface because coalitions and alliances are never more than marriages of convenience. Western Europe again will seek to counterbalance U.S. "hyperpower." The Europeans, Russia, and China will oppose U.S. missile defense deployment. Russia will be suspicious of NATO expansion into the Baltic States and the projection of U.S. power into Central Asia. China will continue to pursue its great-power emergence and will contest the United States for supremacy in East Asia. The war on terrorism, in other words, is merely an interlude in international politics, not the harbinger of everlasting global harmony based on acceptance of U.S. primacy.

Although U.S. policymakers have convinced themselves that the United States is a benign hegemon, no such animal exists in international politics. A hegemon is a threat to the security of others simply because it is so powerful. The United States is not immune to the kind of geopolitical blowback experienced by previous hegemonic aspirants. Thus, in a self-help world the United States must perform the strategic equivalent of threading a needle. It cannot abrogate its freedom to act unilaterally to defend its interests, but Washington needs simultaneously to find a grand strategy that reduces fears of U.S. preponderant power, thereby reducing incentives to engage in counterhegemonic balancing directed at the United States. A good starting point is the war on terrorism itself.

Having overthrown the Taliban regime in Afghanistan and rooted out Al Qaeda terrorists based there, sentiment is strong in the Bush administration, Congress, and the foreign policy establishment for settling the Gulf War's unfinished business by toppling Hussein. Opponents of this policy advance military and diplomatic arguments for caution. The military argument is easily dismissed. Given enormous U.S. military superiority, a war against Iraq would be a cakewalk for the United States. The diplomatic argument—that the antiterror coalition would fragment—is somewhat more serious. Undoubtedly, if the United States launches a full-scale war against Iraq, most, if not all, U.S. Middle Eastern clients would defect from the coalition. Although the alliance's collapse would cause practical military-logistic reasons for concern (to replay the Gulf War, the United States would need ports of entry and staging bases contiguous to Iraq), the abstract goal of preserving the coalition for its own sake should not prevent the United States from confronting Iraq. After all, coalitions and alliances are a means to an end, not an end in themselves. Another diplomatic concern is the possibility of an anti-U.S. backlash in the Islamic world. This worry cannot be dismissed so easily, even though in both the Gulf War and, at least to this point, in the war on terrorism, fears of massive Islamic opposition to U.S. policy have not materialized. Still, the possibility of a strong reaction against the United States must be taken into account.

Those who advocate a hard-line policy toward Iraq seldom consider one other concern. What would happen to Iraq once Hussein was removed from power? A post-Hussein Iraq is not going to be a liberal, Western-style democracy. That a successor regime ultimately would prove more pliable than the current one is not guaranteed. If Hussein were removed, however, the possibility always exists that Iraq would fragment, an outcome that could further destabilize the region. Certainly, the United States does not want to end up "owning" Iraq and being saddled with the difficult and probably dangerous job of imposing a new government there.[17]

Avoiding a full-scale war against Iraq does not mean that Washington should stand aside and allow Hussein to develop weapons of mass destruction and support terrorists. Instead of using a sledgehammer approach, the United States could use a focused, finely calibrated strategy to remove Iraqi threats to U.S. security. Washington's goal should be to remove the sources of threat. It does not have to force a regime change, which would open a geopolitical Pandora's box, to achieve that goal. As U.S. experiences in Kosovo and Afghanistan have demonstrated, if the

United States has good intelligence about where key targets are located, those targets can be destroyed in precision air and missile strikes. Moreover, by developing a full range of intelligence and covert operational capabilities, the United States can sabotage Iraq's (or any other hostile state's) weapons of mass destruction program by interdicting the inflow of key components and materials, destroying plants and research facilities, and eliminating the scientists and engineers without whose expertise such weapons could not be developed. Dealing with the Iraqi problem in this manner would be a much better strategy for the United States because, by reducing its geopolitical footprint in the Middle East, Washington would reduce substantially the dangers that U.S. policy could trigger an antihegemonic backlash.

Changing U.S. Grand Strategy to Reflect the Times

In the longer term, regardless of future developments in the war on terrorism, the paradox of U.S. power will not disappear. Looking beyond the war, the big question confronting U.S. strategists in coming years is how to reduce the risks of U.S. hegemony. To lower the risk, the United States must change its grand strategy. One grand strategic alternative to primacy is offshore balancing.[18]

Like primacy, offshore balancing is a strategy firmly rooted in the Realist tradition. Primacy adherents regard multipolarity—an international system comprised of three or more great powers—as a strategic threat to the United States, while offshore balancers see it as a strategic opportunity for the United States. Offshore balancing is predicated on the assumption that attempting to maintain U.S. hegemony is self-defeating because it will provoke other states to combine in opposition to the United States and result in the futile depletion of the United States' relative power, thereby leaving it worse off than if it accommodated multipolarity. Offshore balancing accepts that the United States cannot prevent the rise of new great powers either within (the EU, Germany, and Japan) or outside (China, a resurgent Russia) its sphere of influence. Offshore balancing would also relieve the United States of its burden of managing the security affairs of turbulent regions such as the Persian Gulf/Middle East and Southeast Europe.

Offshore balancing is a grand strategy based on burden shifting, not burden sharing. It would transfer to others the task of maintaining regional power balances; checking the rise of potential global and regional hegemons; and stabilizing Europe, East Asia, and the Persian Gulf/Middle East. In other words, other states would have to become responsible for providing their own security and for the security of the regions in which they live (and contiguous ones), rather than looking to the United States to do it for them.

The events of September 11 make offshore balancing an attractive grand strategic alternative to primacy for two reasons. First, looking beyond the war on terrorism, the Persian Gulf/Middle East region is clearly, endemically unstable. If the United States attempts to perpetuate its hegemonic role in the region after having accomplished its immediate war aims, the probability of a serious geopolitical backlash within the region against the United States is high. Second, because the U.S. victory in the war on terrorism will underscore U.S. predominance in international politics, victory's paradoxical effect will be to heighten European, Russian, and Chinese fears of U.S. power. By adopting an offshore balancing strategy once the war on terrorism ends, the United States would benefit in two ways.

First, others have much greater intrinsic strategic interests in the region than does the United States. For example, Western Europe, Japan, and, increasingly, China are far more dependent on the region's oil than the United States. Because they live next door, Russia, China, Iran, and India have a much greater long-term security interest in regional stability in the Persian Gulf/Middle East than the United States. By passing the mantle of regional stabilizer to these great and regional powers, the United States could extricate itself from the messy and dangerous geopolitics of the Persian Gulf/Middle East and take itself out of radical Islam's line of fire.

Second, although a competitive component to U.S. relations with the other great powers in a multipolar world would be inescapable, multipolar politics have historically engendered periods of great-power cooperation. On the cooperative side, an offshore balancing strategy would be coupled with a policy of spheres of influence, which have always been an important item in the toolbox of great-power policymakers. By recognizing each other's paramount interests in certain regions, great powers can avoid the kinds of misunderstandings that could trigger conflict. Moreover, the mere act of signaling that one country understands another's larger security stake in a particular region, a stake that it will respect by noninterference, allows states to communicate a nonthreatening posture to one another. By recognizing the legitimacy of other interests, a great power also signals that it accepts them as equals. An offshore balancing strategy would immunize the United States against a post–war-on-terrorism backlash against U.S. hegemony in one other way. By accepting the emergence of new great powers and simultaneously pulling back from its primacy-driven military posture, the United States would reduce perception of a "U.S. threat," thereby lowering the chances that others will view it as an overpowerful hegemon. In this sense, offshore balancing is a strategy of restraint that would allow the United States to minimize the risks of open confrontation with the new great powers.

Being Panglossian about the reemergence of multipolarity in international politics would be silly. Multipolarity is not the best outcome imaginable. The best outcome would be a world in which every other state willingly accepted U.S. hegemony—an outcome about which some may dream, but one that will never be realized in the real world. That outcome, however, is much better than the predictable outcome if the United States continues to follow a grand strategy of primacy. The outcome of that strategy will be really bad: not only will new great powers rise, they will also coalesce against what they perceive to be a U.S. threat.

Notwithstanding the events of September 11, U.S. hegemony is the salient fact that defines the U.S. role in international politics. The articles in "Through the Looking Glass" reflect a deep mistrust of U.S. power that the temporary convergence of interests brought about by the war on terrorism will not wash away. Indeed, the reverse is true. In attaining victory in the war's opening round, the United States under-lined its dominant role in the international system, and talk of a "new U.S. empire" echoes inside the beltway. Underscoring the paradox of U.S. power is the paradox of victory. Flushed with triumph and the awesome display of U.S. might, U.S. policymakers may succumb to hu-bris and overreach strategically in the false belief that U.S. hegemony is an unchallengeable fact of international life. Other states, however, will draw the opposite conclusion: that the United States is too powerful and that its hegemony must be resisted. Now, more than ever, having a great debate about future U.S. grand strategy is imperative. As that de-bate unfolds, offshore balancing will become the obvious successor strategy to primacy because it is a grand strategic escape hatch by which the United States can avoid the fate that has befallen previous hegemons in modern international history.

Notes

1. Chong Guan Kwa and See Seng Tan, "The Keystone of World Order," *The Washington Quarterly* 24, no. 3 (summer 2001): 99.

2. Wu Xinbo, "To Be an Enlightened Superpower," *The Washington Quarterly* 24, no. 3 (summer 2001): 63–71; Dimitri Trenin, "Less Is More," *The Washington Quarterly* 24, no. 3 (summer 2001): 135–44.

3. Pascal Boniface, "The Specter of Unilateralism," *The Washington Quarterly* 24, no. 3 (summer 2001): 155–62; Peter Ludlow, "Wanted: A Global Partner," *The Washington Quarterly* 24, no. 3 (summer 2001): 163–71; Michael Stürmer, "Balance from Beyond the Sea," *The Washington Quarterly* 24, no. 3 (summer 2001): 145–53; Akio Watanabe, "First among Equals," *The Washington Quarterly* 24, no. 3 (summer 2001): 73–81.

4. See Pamela Constable, "Anti-American Sentiment Spreading in Pakistan," *Washington Post*, October 15, 2001, p. A1; Barry Bearak, "In Pakistan, a Shaky Ally," *New York Times*, October 2, 2001.

5. Joseph Kahn, "U.S. Is Planning an Aid Package for Pakistan Worth Billions," *New York Times*, October 27, 2001.

6. Joseph Kahn, "I.M.F. Bankers Get Ready to Give Pakistan a Loan," *New York Times*, September 20, 2001.

7. T. R. Reid and William Drozdiak, "Allies Express Solidarity and Caution," *Washington Post*, September 22, 2001, p. A19; Patrick E. Tyler and Jane Perlez,

"World Leaders List Conditions on Cooperation," *New York Times*, September 19, 2001; Suzanne Daley, "A Pause to Ponder Washington's Tough Talk," *New York Times*, September 16, 2001.

8. Richard Boudreaux, "A Superpower's Sorrow, Comeuppance," *Los Angeles Times*, September 13, 2001.

9. For many of the key articles on U.S. grand strategy published during the past decade, see Michael E. Brown et al., *America's Strategic Choices* (Cambridge, Mass.: MIT Press, 2000).

10. Charles Krauthammer, "The Unipolar Moment," *Foreign Affairs: America and the World* 70, no. 1 (1990/1991): 23–33.

11. For extended discussion of the argument made in this paragraph, see Christopher Layne, "The Unipolar Illusion: Why New Great Powers Will Rise," *International Security* 17, no. 4 (spring 1993): 5–51.

12. Henry A. Kissinger, "The Long Shadow of Vietnam," *Newsweek*, May 1, 2000, p. 50.

13. Sandy R. Berger, "American Power," speech, fall 1999 (given while President Bill Clinton's national security adviser). The speech was posted during the Clinton administration on the Web site for the National Security Council.

14. Christopher Layne, "What's Built Up Must Come Down," *Washington Post*, November 4, 1999, p. B1.

15. Richard K. Betts, "The New Threat of Mass Destruction," *Foreign Affairs* 77, no. 1 (January/February 1998): 41.

16. John J. Mearsheimer, *The Tragedy of Great Power Politics* (New York: W. W. Norton, 2001), p. 33.

17. See Dan Byman, "Iraq after Saddam," *The Washington Quarterly* 24, no. 4 (autumn 2001): 151–162.

18. For fuller descriptions of offshore balancing, see Benjamin Schwarz and Christopher Layne, "A New Grand Strategy," *Atlantic Monthly* 289, no. 1 (January 2002): 36–42; Christopher Layne, "From Preponderance to Offshore Balancing: America's Future Grand Strategy," *International Security* 22, no. 1 (summer 1997): 86–124; Christopher Layne, "American Grand Strategy after the Cold War: Primacy or Blue Water?" in Charles F. Hermann, ed., *American Defense Annual 1994* (New York: Lexington, 1994), pp. 19–43; Layne, "The Unipolar Illusion," pp. 45–51. See generally Mearsheimer, *The Tragedy of Great Power Politics* (especially chapters 7 and 8).

Steven E. Miller

The End of Unilateralism or Unilateralism Redux?

The terrorist attacks of September 11 will scythe through history, separating a naively complacent past from a frighteningly vulnerable future. In one stunning strike, highly motivated but ultimately weak and stateless actors painfully wounded the impregnable hegemon. Almost immediately, this event was perceived as epochal, demarcating the passage from one world to another. Many media commentators have portentously proclaimed it as "the day that everything changed."

What did this event mean for U.S. foreign policy? Will this rent in the fabric of history produce large discontinuities in Washington's external behavior? Most (although not all) of the commentary since September 11 has focused on the new realities that seem ineluctably to demand major alterations in U.S. foreign policy. Many now hope, presume, expect, predict, recommend, or in some cases fear and regret that U.S. policy must change dramatically to accommodate the exigencies of the war against terrorism. Many of the United States' friends and allies abroad and many critics at home have rushed to assert that policies and approaches long regarded as objectionable are now entirely unsuitable to the needs of the new international situation. Above all, many have

Steven E. Miller is director of the International Security Program, Belfer Center for Science and International Affairs, at the John F. Kennedy School of Government, Harvard University.

Copyright © 2001 by The Center for Strategic and International Studies and the Massachusetts Institute of Technology
The Washington Quarterly • 25:1 pp. 15–29.

What Does the World Want from America?

claimed that September 11 and its aftermath must spell the end of U.S. unilateralism, which had reached its apogee in the first months of the Bush administration: "[t]he specter of unilateralism" should be regarded as a thing of the past.[1] Such views are understandable, but they may be mistaken. The very real pressures for change in U.S. policy may not be as powerful or as inevitable as many seem to believe.

Four factors suggest that U.S. policy may change in large, visible, and perhaps even fundamental ways. First, and most obviously, Washington's priorities have changed. The war against terrorism will take precedence over all else. Indeed, President George W. Bush is reported to believe that his presidency will be judged according to the effectiveness with which he wages this war. He has become, as one account put it, the leader with no time for the plans of September 10.[2] The items at the top of the foreign policy agenda on September 10—missile defense and NATO enlargement, for example—have faded in prominence and importance and will no longer be the primary focus of high-level attention and energy. Favored policies of the past will be subordinated to the needs of an effective campaign against terrorism.

Second, the Bush administration is now subject to the constraints associated with forging an international coalition against terrorism. It will want the widest possible international support for its war. It will need the active cooperation of at least some other states if it is to prosecute this war in an effective fashion. It will depend on unprecedented international sharing of intelligence for its vision of a relentless, long-term campaign against global terrorism to meet with success. The requirements of international collaboration may temper Washington's unilateralist impulses and compel greater acknowledgement of the interests and perceptions of others.

Third, Washington may now be motivated to address the root causes of terrorism, or at least to address the socioeconomic conditions that produce foot soldiers for the terrorist cause and that lead populations to support the terrorists. This possibility implies efforts to resolve festering conflicts whose ongoing, embittering violence and bloodshed breeds fanaticism. It also implies a need to raise impoverished populations out of squalor, deprivation, and economic hopelessness; prosperity, it is thought, produces few suicide bombers. The attacks of September 11 suggest that ignoring the world's troubles and the world's trouble spots is perilous. If conflict and deprivation produce terrorism, then ignoring those circumstances where conflict and deprivation reign is dangerous for the United States. Many believe an enlightened long-term strategy for fighting terrorism will include efforts to eliminate the conditions that breed terrorists in the first place. Indeed, this approach may be the only truly effective long-run strategy for eliminating the terrorist threat to the United States. The notion of "nation-building" has inspired contempt in Washington and had been explicitly rejected by the Bush administration, but something like it is a potentially key element of a strategy to combat terrorism. The construction of stable polities with reasonably successful economies in places where failed states now exist may be a prerequisite to long-term success in eliminating terrorism.

Finally, the attacks on September 11 clearly demonstrated that the cost of U.S. involvement abroad can be extraordinarily high. This painful exhibition might produce (and many believe it should produce) a recalculation of the costs and benefits of an activist, internationalist foreign policy in general or of specific regional policies in particular. This recalculation could suggest a lower profile in some contexts and a higher profile in others (more efforts to resolve chronic conflicts, for example). Some military deployments overseas, such as that of the U.S. forces in Saudi Arabia, which so enrages Osama bin Laden, will now look more risky and may seem less advisable. The U.S. propensity to poke its nose in others' affairs, and especially in others' conflicts, may weaken, given that the potential costs of doing so are understood to be so high. Washington's willingness to bear costs, run risks, and shoulder political burdens on behalf of friends and allies may attenuate. The example of Israel is commonly cited; many believe that U.S. support for Israel "makes America itself a target of Muslim rage."[3] In the future, Washington may well wish to find policies that reduce its exposure to the dangerous rages of others. This desire need not imply, in the case of

Israel or others, a reversal of policy or a complete abandonment of past commitments, but a certain amount of reappraisal and redirection would not be surprising.[4] In the short run, of course, no one will want to take steps that appear to be capitulations to terrorism or that appear to imply that U.S. policy is ultimately to blame for outrageous acts of terrorism. Many believe that over time, however, the United States may want to reconsider those policies that are thought to raise the risk of further terrorist attacks. Now that the potential price tag of such policies has been vividly demonstrated, alternatives may seem both more feasible and more attractive.

Taken together, these considerations lead rather readily to the conclusion that U.S. foreign policy must change significantly and, indeed, that such change is imperative given the obvious magnitude of the terrorist threat. Many commentators are offering their thoughts about what Washington can do, should do, and must do to make its foreign policy relevant and effective in the aftermath of September 11.[5] A common judgment is that the events of September 11 should mean the end of U.S. unilateralism. Many hope and recommend that the pronounced unilateralist tendencies evident in the first months of the Bush administration will now be jettisoned in the cause of fighting terrorism. Washington must surely understand now that the United States cannot go it alone, that it needs allies and partners in the struggle against terrorism.[6]

Similarly, fears that the next large-scale terrorist attack might involve nuclear, chemical, or biological weapons are thought to highlight the importance of preserving and strengthening existing international regimes constraining traffic in such weapons and materials—despite the well-documented skepticism of the Bush administration toward such regimes. Further, many believe that the United States should, and will, abandon or set aside controversial policies that may interfere with building a wide international coalition for the campaign against terrorism—especially policies that affront the interests or sensibilities of particularly important potential partners. Thus, sanctions on Pakistan are now extremely awkward and inconvenient. U.S. distaste for the more brutal aspects of the Uzbek regime will now take a backseat to the need to obtain Uzbekistan's help in support of the military operations in Afghanistan. The importance of Russian cooperation in the campaign against bin Laden and the Taliban puts a whole series of major issues—Chechnya, missile defense, NATO enlargement, Russian relations with its southern neighbors, and economic assistance—in a completely different context. The United States may want to make more of an effort to satisfy the wishes and preferences of its European allies now that it seeks to enlist their support in a long global struggle against terrorism.[7]

Even a brief consideration of these four factors clearly reveals why so many commentators conclude that significant alterations of U.S. foreign policy are necessary, likely, or inevitable. The campaign against terrorism will impose new demands on U.S. diplomacy. Changes in U.S. policy will be discernible. Indeed, this line of thought has received validation in the behavior of the Bush administration in the first weeks after the September 11 attacks. The administration has worked diligently, patiently, and effectively to attract international support for its antiterrorist policies and to gain at least the minimum necessary assent from key states such as Russia, Pakistan, and Saudi Arabia.

In short, the factors promoting change in U.S. foreign policy are clear and potent, and many within and outside the U.S. government embrace them. In the shocked, grief-filled early weeks after the attacks, however, the tendency has been to ignore, overlook, or undervalue arguments and factors suggesting that many of the main U.S. priorities and policies could remain intact even in an era shaped by the events of September 11. As the horrible events of September 11 recede into the past, normal politics will gradually resurface. Changes in U.S. policy still quite possibly may not be as broad, dramatic, profound, or enduring as many seem to expect or to recommend.

The most common and most sweeping set of claims about why U.S. foreign policy should be set on a new course after September 11 involves the requirements of building a coalition. The argument, in essence, suggests that the Bush administration will be forced to modify or abandon many of its previous policies in order to build the necessary coalition to fight terrorism. This argument has merit but is less power-ful than is often assumed.

Does the Lone Ranger Need a Posse?

The United States would certainly welcome and prefer the widest pos-sible international support as it undertakes its war against terrorism. Whether Washington believes that significant adjustments in its inter-national policies are necessary in order to attract that wide support, however, is far from clear. On the contrary, Washington seems to as-sume and expect that most of the world will join what it sees as a struggle between good and evil. Bush said plainly in his forceful address to the Congress, "Either you're with us, or you're with the terrorists."

This thought has echoed among the Washington elite. In a speech shortly after the attack, for example, former house speaker Newt Gingrich commented, "There are only two teams on the planet for this war. There's the team that represents civilization and there's the team that represents terrorism. Just tell us which. There are no neutrals."[8] Such rhetoric is not enticing but threatening, not accommodating but uncom-promising. The message is not that the United States will bend and shift in order to attract support but that those who choose to join the other side will be sorry. Moreover, those who join the U.S. team are clearly ex-pected to follow the U.S. lead; Washington intends to call the shots. As one commentator put it, "Bush has won extensive support for his with-us-or-against-us approach to terrorism, [but] he is quietly enforcing the subtext that there is only one captain and one playbook for the team he has formed."[9] This rhetoric is not the stuff of a new multilateralism.

Political support for Washington is generally assumed, if not demanded; military contributions from others are in general neither sought nor needed. Of course, the United States needs overflight rights and stag-ing areas in South or Central Asia in order to conduct military opera-tions against the Taliban and bin Laden in Afghanistan. The United States is not, however, mobilizing, and does not need to mobilize, a great coalition war machine to conduct this campaign. Indeed, in recent wars, allied military contributions have been politically expedient but operationally inconvenient—and they come at the cost of giving allies a complicating voice in the councils of war. More than any other state, the United States is able to operate militarily as a lone ranger (perhaps with Great Britain in the role of trusty sidekick). Its surfeit of military power gives it the luxury to operate from a position of superiority against any conceivable opponent, and its long-range striking power gives it unilateral military options available to no other state. Not all political problems are amenable to military solutions, but from a military perspective the United States does not need to renovate its foreign policy in order to assemble a large coalition of fighting forces.

Some will argue that, regardless, the campaign against terrorism requiring extensive international intelligence collaboration is an inescapable fact. The United States cannot joust effectively with the global terrorist threat while relying solely on its own intelligence resources, particularly in those reaches of the earth where U.S. intelligence is almost surely incomplete, inadequate, or inferior to intelligence in the possession of other states. Thus, arguably, the intelligence requirements of the war against terrorism will compel the United States to build a meaningful international coalition and to pay the diplomatic price for doing so. Perhaps this consideration will trigger large and long-term changes in U.S. foreign policy.

No one can dispute that the campaign against terrorism will profit from the accumulation of relevant information from as many useful sources as are available. In the aftermath of September 11, additional information from additional sources will likely contribute to operations against terrorism. Nevertheless, for several reasons, this factor may have been exaggerated as a motivation for fundamental change in U.S. policy.

For one thing, the barriers to intensive intelligence collaboration are considerable. U.S. agencies are reluctant to share information with each other, much less with foreign governments and foreign intelligence bureaucracies. When sensitive information is involved, the police are out of the loop, Congress is eyed warily, and other federal agencies are not routinely on the distribution list.[10] Assessing the intimacy of information-sharing arrangements between governments is impossible for outsiders, but intelligence professionals suggest that the United States does not share everything even with its closest allies and that even states with close ties to the United States may not be enthusiastic or generous about turning over information to their U.S. counterparts. Washington was deeply frustrated, for example, that the government of Saudi Arabia was not more forthcoming in assisting the investigation of the 1996 terrorist attack on U.S. military personnel at Khobar Towers.

Moreover, the current loose coalition that has formed in support of the U.S. battle with terrorism includes a motley collection of states—some that are close to the United States but many that are not. Indeed, many of the states that might be in the best position to possess and provide information about terrorist activities in the Middle East or South Asia—such as Iran, Libya, and Syria—are states that have uneasy, or even hostile, relations with the United States. The barriers to collaboration must be enormous in such cases, with reluctance likely in both directions to forging the most sensitive sorts of ties between unfriendly states. In circumstances where deep trust between governments does not exist, concerns will inevitably arise that information is being manipulated, withheld, parceled out to maximize the price, shaded to advance the interests of the providing state, or even falsely manufactured.[11] When genuine and useful information is provided, it may reflect only partial truths or be misleading and self-serving in some way. In its quest to crush the global terrorist threat, the United States will probably seek information from whatever sources can provide it, but will the United States truly be prepared to pay a high price in terms of its foreign policy in order to gain problematic information from dubious sources?

On the other hand, strong intelligence ties with allies (such as NATO) and close friends (such as Israel) already exist. In these cases, a pattern of extensive intelligence collaboration and information-sharing is long established. Limits to cooperation exist even in these contexts (NATO's vast bureaucracy is notoriously porous regarding information, for example), but Washington currently enjoys whatever advantages derive from this intelligence collaboration. The United States may wish to point these collaborative efforts more directly at the terrorist threat and to utilize existing networks in different ways (such as rounding up terrorist suspects residing in allied countries). U.S. foreign policy reform, however, does not need to occur in order for the United States to gain the benefits of intelligence cooperation with long-time friends and allies. In short, although the United States will want and need international help and support in its war against terrorism, assuming that the demands of coalition-building will inevitably compel Washington to alter course dramatically, to reverse unpopular lines of policy, or to abandon past priorities is a mistake.

The Coalition Blues

This judgment is reinforced when one considers the origins and character of the global coalition that has formed against terrorism. Particularly if the Bush administration persists with the objective of mounting a relentless, long-term campaign against terrorism, no one will be surprised that Washington will find tending the antiterrorist coalition to be frustrating and burdensome. How much time will pass before Washington sings the coalition blues?

The origins of the global alignment against terrorism lay not in considered calculations of interest or careful articulations of positions but in gut reactions to the events of September 11. The terrorist attacks in New York and Washington were, among other things, an international CNN special. Around the world, people were glued to their television sets, many of them watching live as the aircraft struck the second tower at the World Trade Center, as desperate souls flung themselves out of windows from the upper floors of 110-story buildings, and as the towers collapsed. Anyone who missed seeing the action as it happened would have countless opportunities to view the scenes as the video footage played over and over again. The raw human emotion that these events produced was widely shared. People the world over felt revulsion at what they had witnessed.

Initial diplomatic reactions reflected this emotional impact. Most governments quickly condemned the terror, conveyed condolences to the U.S. people, and offered generic support to the United States in its battle with terrorism. Indeed, only a handful of states failed to condemn the attacks. U.S. friends and allies (many of whom lost citizens in the attack on the World Trade Center) lined up beside Washington. NATO rapidly invoked Article 5 of the North Atlantic Treaty: an attack on one is an attack on all. Expressions of sympathy and support poured in from quarters expected and unexpected.

Thus, within a few days, an almost universal rhetorical coalition against terrorism existed. For the majority of states that had no directly relevant role in the battle ahead, embracing this position simply meant joining the forces of civilization and avoiding the ire of the United States while raising little risk that something difficult or costly would be demanded of them. Yet for quite a number of other states—U.S. allies in NATO, U.S. friends and allies in the Islamic world, those nations relevant or useful in one way or another to the struggle against terrorism—commitment to this cause could result in the need to make painful decisions, take costly actions, and suffer unhappy consequences. Hence, the undoubtedly genuine solidarity that such states felt was soon accompanied by caveats and second thoughts; they are with the United States in this fight but not unconditionally.[12] Even the NATO allies in Europe, having swiftly taken the unprecedented step of invoking Article 5, were then palpably uneasy about what the United States might do with the blank check it might think it now possessed (and were palpably relieved when the United States did not undertake rapid, impulsive, excessive, or reckless military retaliation).

Finally, for a much smaller group of states—including Pakistan, Saudi Arabia, Russia, and Uzbekistan—that are politically or logistically crucial to the U.S. response to the September 11 attacks, collaboration with the United States was inevitably a major step, one that could raise both excruciating risks and lucrative opportunities. For states such as Pakistan or Saudi Arabia, striking the right balance between the political or practical needs of the United States, the demands of their own populations as well as their own domestic political circumstances, and fears of provoking terrorist attacks on their own regimes is no small challenge. The costs of cooperation could be very large. A flat refusal to cooperate with Washington, however, would be extremely damaging, producing a wrathful United States that would undoubtedly still find ways to prosecute its desired retaliation and to punish those who had refused to help. Day by day, one can watch Islamabad and Riyadh agonizingly walk this tightrope, as they try to satisfy the United States with enough support while trying to minimize the costs of doing so. Thus Pakistan's president, General Pervez Musharraf, voiced support for the U.S. bombings in Afghanistan but also expressed the hope that the strikes would be over quickly and that they would be limited to military targets. The Saudi government has articulated sympathy for the U.S. antiterrorist efforts but has been unwilling to take every action that the United States has requested.[13]

For these truly crucial states, however, alignment with the United States is not only a matter of running risks and bearing costs; they are also in a position to exact a price. The more difficulty they have in fulfilling Washington's demands and the more genuinely reluctant or ambivalent they are, the stronger their bargaining position will be. Russia, for example, has facilitated U.S. access to Central Asia, may possess useful intelligence about Afghanistan, and can contribute to the fight against the Taliban. Moscow's support is thought to be essential. Suddenly, Moscow possesses some unexpected bargaining leverage in its relations with the United States. One unnamed Russian was quoted as saying that the events of September 11 "are so advantageous to the Russian government, you might think they did it themselves."[14] Having joined the U.S. coalition and having provided valuable help, Moscow is likely to expect greater understanding for its own, self-styled war against terrorism in Chechnya; less pressure from the United States over issues such as missile defense and NATO expansion; and perhaps more generosity from Western financial institutions.

Similarly, access to Pakistan's air space and territory are essential if the United States is to conduct effective military actions in or against Afghanistan, especially against the Taliban strongholds in southeast Afghanistan. Islamabad's fairly prompt acquiescence—despite the fragility of the Pakistani government, despite the support for bin Laden among its own populous, and despite its own involvement with the Taliban—was almost immediately rewarded. Barely 10 days after the September 11 attacks, Bush announced that he would lift the economic sanctions imposed on Pakistan after its nuclear tests in May 1998. Soon thereafter, the United States made public the preparation of a major aid package for Pakistan, worth hundreds of millions of dollars, and expressed its support for international financial institutions' provision of debt relief for Islamabad.[15] For its part, Uzbekistan has sought security assurances as well as economic assistance in return for the use of its territory as a staging area for U.S. military power.[16] Washington is learning, once again, that there is no getting without giving. Worth noting, however, is that the United States is getting what it needs from these states through a series of specific bilateral transactions that have no particular bearing on whether U.S. foreign policy in general is moving away from unilateralism.

This coalition is clearly of a different sort (if it is a coalition at all), one whose broadest manifestation consists of nothing more than a willingness at the rhetorical level to condemn terrorism. It brings together an unnatural constellation of states, some that at their base share little more than a desire to prevent damage to their relationship with the United States and some that will have little to do with one another. It may include states that are generally unfriendly toward the United States or, in the most amazing instances, states that are on the U.S. list of state sponsors of terrorism.[17] Indeed, some key coalition "partners," such as Pakistan and Saudi Arabia, are states that are deeply implicated in the rise of Islamic terrorism.[18]

Among those nations prepared to play an active role in the fight, many are prepared to stand with the United States only in limited ways. Some are grudging or reluctant participants in the coalition, feeling that they have no choice but to go along with the United States while harboring no real passion for the cause and having no reason to run great risks. Some key participants have powerful incentives to tread cautiously and to circumscribe their roles as much as possible because the potential costs to them of entanglement with the United States are enormous. Some are willing to cooperate, provided the rewards are large enough. Some key states in Central and South Asia are fragile and politically unstable, raising the risk that U.S. military activities in the region "could turn the area into a shatter zone of collapsing states."[19] This coalition is not NATO writ large. It is not a collection of states bound by common values or a tight alliance forged by the binding effects of a large common threat. It is a mélange of states hastily assembled through insistent U.S. diplomatic maneuverings for the immediate purpose of facilitating U.S. retaliation in Afghanistan and for the longer-term purpose of facilitating the U.S. campaign against terrorism.

This coalition will not be easy for Washington to preserve or manage. No other state has quite the same stake in this fight as does the United States. Other states inevitably will have and will act on their own interests, perceptions, preferences, and constraints. As the emotions associated with the September 11 tragedy diminish, differences are likely to become more visible. As politics as usual regains force, others will likely be more willing to voice their contrary views. As the war against terrorism unfolds, the United States is bound to make missteps and to take actions with unfortunate, undesired consequences—the accidental killing of civilians, for example—that provoke criticism, weaken support, and undermine the U.S. position.

The Bush administration appears to be utterly resolved to wage the war against terrorism indefinitely, but the commitment of others is likely to wane. Indeed, not much more than a week after air strikes commenced in Afghanistan, Washington's partners may already have been losing their patience with U.S. military operations.[20] Washington is likely to view the coalition as a source of support and an instrument of U.S. policy, but others are likely to see it as a mechanism for influencing U.S. decisions or restraining U.S. action—a possibility that is mirrored in Bush administration concerns that the coalition might "shackle" the United States.[21] Further, the United States will not find it easy to push its coalition partners to do things they do not want to do or feel that they cannot do. Managing this coalition will be a demanding, messy, vexing, and occasionally fruitless exercise.

The United States will undoubtedly continue the diplomatic maneuverings it thinks are necessary or desirable to permit and support its war against terrorism. This ungainly coalition, however, if it will be a true coalition, is unlikely to be so potent or so appealing an instrument that Washington is certain to sacrifice other policies comprehensively for its sake.

How Much Change, by Whom, in What Directions?

One great reversal has emerged from this crisis: restoring foreign policy to the high table of U.S. politics. Of course, consequential foreign and security policy issues were on the agenda prior to September 11, but the public was largely indifferent to external affairs. The president's primary interests and priorities lay elsewhere—in tax cuts and educational reform, among other things. The preoccupying debates involved budget deficits and surpluses, Social Security funding, tax rebates, economic policy, and so on. Now, the aftermath of September 11 has captivated the entire U.S. political scene. The terrorist threat, the war against terrorism, and the diplomatic repercussions of fighting terrorism are now the dominant public concerns and will remain so for a long time to come. This issue has swamped all others. By all accounts, since the terrorist attacks, Bush has focused on little else.

Many also believe and recommend that the events of September 11 should produce a series of policy reversals. New forces are now shaping U.S. foreign policy, which policymakers need to recast to reflect the centrality of the fight against terrorism. The lone hegemon, indulging its unilateralist instincts, cannot wage an effective global war on terrorism. The unrivaled military superpower cannot, by arms alone, protect itself from the violence and fanaticism of the weak and the dispossessed. The myopic giant, focusing on its own priorities and deaf to the interests and the preferences of others, cannot assemble and sustain a wide international coalition against terrorism. The arrogant hyperpower, so suspicious of international regimes and institutions, cannot effectively utilize these instruments in the battle against terrorism while also criticizing, undermining, or rejecting them. Washington, in short, will need to change its ways, adopting a foreign policy more suited to the war it is now waging.

From this logic flows a series of conclusions about what the United States should do. At the most general level, it should move from unilateralism to multilateralism. It should shift from criticizing international institutions to building and utilizing them, from doubting and rejecting international restraint regimes to strengthening them. It should recognize the importance of nation-building and conflict resolution to suppress the terrorist threat. It should alter or abandon policies that interfere with the creation and functioning of the antiterrorist coalition or that make the United States a target for terrorism. These requirements, it is commonly argued, are the imperatives of the age of terror.

Powerful forces for change in U.S. policy unquestionably now exist. The real issue is whether the United States will respond to these forces in the ways that so many—friends, allies, pundits, and specialists— think it should. No one has any reason to assume that the United States will inevitably move in these directions. Certainly, changes in U.S. policy have occurred and will occur, and some of these changes will be consistent with what others think Washington should now do. The record is likely to be at best mixed, however, and advocates of sweeping policy reversals are likely to be disappointed.

The antiterrorist coalition is neither so necessary nor so valuable as to make those who set U.S. policy likely to alter fundamental beliefs about international politics or abandon deeply rooted policy priorities. Although Russia is a crucial player, for example, the Bush administration has not sought to reassure it about other contentious issues such as missile defense or NATO enlargement. On the contrary, even after September 11, Washington has pointedly reaffirmed its commitment to those policies.[22] Similarly, the Bush administration has welcomed supportive resolutions from the United Nations (UN) General Assembly, but it insists that it does not require authorization from the UN in order to act.[23] No indications exist that the Bush administration has changed its mind or altered its position on the Kyoto Protocol, the Comprehensive Test Ban Treaty, the International Criminal Court, the Biological Weapons Convention, or on any of the other issues where its opposition and recalcitrance have given U.S. policy its unilateralist flavor. Nor is there strong evidence that Washington believes its strategy for the antiterrorist campaign must completely avoid options and policies distasteful to others. For example, war with Iraq is very much on the agenda of possibilities in Washington, although it inspires enthusiasm almost nowhere else.

The Bush administration will make its choices and pay the price for the support it truly needs. It will do what it must and be prepared, as former CIA director James Woolsey has urged, "to put up with criticism from European governments and other states."[24] It will take the steps it thinks are necessary and expect its friends and allies to stand with the forces of civilization against the global blight of terrorism. It may be, indeed, that the lonely hegemon expects others to adapt to its needs and preferences rather than the other way around, especially now that it is at war. Even in these new circumstances, the United States may not be able to resist "the itch of unilateralism."[25]

Notes

1. Pascal Boniface, "The Specter of Unilateralism," *Washington Quarterly* 24, no. 3 (summer 2001): 155–162.

2. David Sanger and Elisabeth Bumiller, "In One Month, a Presidency Is Transformed," *New York Times*, October 11, 2001.

3. "America and Israel: The Unblessed Peacemaker," *Economist*, October 6, 2001, p. 19. Notably, though, bin Laden himself does not appear to be strongly motivated by considerations related to the Arab-Israeli dispute.

4. See Joseph Nye, "The Limits of Change," *Financial Times*, September 14, 2001 (urging greater U.S. involvement in the Middle East peace process as one appropriate response to the terrorist attacks).

5. Stephen Walt, "Foreign Affairs—Fragile: Package with Care," *Boston Globe*, September 30, 2001.

6. See Moises Naim, "Even a Hegemon Needs Friends and Allies," *Financial Times*, September 14, 2001; Francis Fukuyama, "The United State," *Financial Times*, September 15–16, 2001.

7. For an expression of Europe's hopes and preferences, see Peter Ludlow, "Wanted: A Global Partner," *Washington Quarterly* 24, no. 3 (summer 2001): 163–171.

8. Nicholas Lemann, "Letter from Washington: The Options," *New Yorker*, October 1, 2001, p. 75. See also R. W. Apple Jr., "Stark Choice from Washington: Ally or Enemy in Global Assault," *International Herald Tribune*, September 15–16, 2001.

9. John Vinocur, "America's 'We'll Call If We Need You' War," *International Herald Tribune*, October 3, 2001.

10. See Michael Isikoff, "The FBI: They're Not Sharing Anything," *Newsweek*, October 15, 2001, p. 6 (relating bitter public complaints from U.S. police departments about the FBI's refusal to share information with them about the investigation of terrorist threats in the United States).

11. See William Safire, "High Cost of Coalition," *New York Times*, October 4, 2001 (warning about paying too much and getting too little in intelligence relationships with other governments).

12. For an excellent illustration of this point, see Patrick Tyler and Jane Perlez, "World Leaders List Conditions on Cooperation," *New York Times*, September 19, 2001.

13. See Jane Perlez, "Shaky Ally: Saudi Cooperation on bin Laden Lags, U.S. Aides Say," *New York Times*, October 11, 2001.

14. Anne Applebaum, "How the World Has Changed, Part 1," *Slate*, September 21, 2001.

15. See Jane Perlez, "Bush Rewarding Pakistan for Its Support; U.S. Plans End for Sanctions on Islamabad," *New York Times*, September 22, 2001; Alan Sipress and Steven Mufson, "U.S. Readies Financial Package for Allies," *Washington Post*, October 2, 2001; Gerald Seib, "Allies' Cooperation in War on Terrorism May Carry a Price Tag of Future Favors," *Wall Street Journal*, September 26, 2001.

16. Susan Glasser, "New Allies Seek Payback," *Washington Post*, October 1, 2001.

17. See Alan Sipress and Steven Mufson, "U.S. Explores Recruiting Iran into New Coalition," *Washington Post*, September 25, 2001.

18. See Robert Scheer, "Who Do We Bomb Next?" *Salon.com*, October 17, 2001, located at www.salon.com (suggesting that, "[i]f President Bush were serious about his stated goal of punishing nations that support terrorism, Saudi Arabia would be the next logical target").

19. Robert D. Kaplan, "A Who's Who for the Next Afghan Regime," *Boston Globe*, October 17, 2001, sec. A, p. 15.

20. June Thomas, "War: What Is It Good For?" *Slate*, October 17, 2001.

21. Steven Mufson, "War Cabinet: Veterans on Familiar Ground," *Washington Post*, October 1, 2001 (quoting Deputy Secretary of Defense Paul Wolfowitz).

See also Richard Lowry, "Strength Is Not in Coalition," *USA Today*, September 20, 2001 ("The [United States] should make certain that the coalition it assembles serves its purposes, and be willing to go it alone if it doesn't. ... The U.S. anti-terrorism drive cannot stall around some Brussels conference table....").

22. See Susan Blasser, "U.S. to Pursue Withdrawal from ABM Pact," *Washington Post*, September 17, 2001; Tom Canahuate, "U.S. Reassures NATO Aspirants on Enlargement," *DefenseNews.com*, September 26, 2001, located at www.defensenews.com/home.php.

23. Nicholas Kralev, "U.S. Can Strike without UN Nod," *Washington Times*, September 27, 2001.

24. Elaine Sciolino and Patrick Tyler, "Some Pentagon Officials and Advisers Seek to Oust Iraq's Leader in War's Next Phase," *New York Times*, October 12, 2001.

25. Stanley Hoffmann, "On the War," *New York Review of Books*, November 1, 2001, p. 6.